Autism and Your Church

Nurturing the Spiritual Growth of People with Autism Spectrum Disorders

BARBARA J. NEWMAN

Friendship
MINISTRIES

Friendship Ministries is an interdenominational, international ministry for people with cognitive impairments. Through consultation and with the help of resources that encourage spiritual development and relationships, Friendship Ministries helps churches to include people with cognitive impairments in fellowship and service as members of the body of Christ.

Friendship Ministries is grateful to the CLC Network for sharing in the development costs of this resource book. A special word of thanks goes to R. H. Berends, executive director of CLC Network.

 CLC Network is an organization dedicated to including persons with disabilities in the fabric of communities. Although its work began in Christian day schools, CLC now offers adults services as well as services to churches who desire assistance in setting up educational programs and support networks (GLUE teams) for people with disabilities.

Illustrations by April Hartmann

Contact Us
We welcome your comments. Call Friendship Ministries toll free at 1-888-866-8966; write to us at 2850 Kalamazoo Ave. SE, Grand Rapids, MI 49560; e-mail us at friendship@friendship.org; or visit www.Friendship.org.

Library of Congress Cataloging-in-Publication Data
Newman, Barbara J., 1962-
  Autism and your church : nurturing the spiritual growth of people with autism spectrum disorders / Barbara J. Newman.–1st ed.
    p. cm.
  ISBN 1-59255-273-0
1. Church work with people with mental disabilities. 2. People with mental disabilities–Religious life. 3. Autism–Religious aspects–Christianity. 4. Autism. 5. Developmental disabilities–Religious aspects–Christianity. I. Title.

BV4461.N49 2006
259'.419685882–dc22

                    2005031711

10 9 8 7 6 5 4 3 2 1

To Mae and Andrew Bandstra, my mom and dad, for your godly
unconditional love and support through all of my years.

You've taught me through a multitude of experiences that the people around us are gifts
from God to be respected and cherished. Thanks for teaching me about God's knitting.

I love you both so much!

Acknowledgments

A resource book is never the result of the work of one individual. God has given each person and organization to me as a gift, and I express my sincere appreciation to

- *Friendship Ministries,* Grand Rapids, Michigan. You have provided the opportunity to develop this resource, and I am blessed by your vision and purpose.
- *CLC Network,* Grand Rapids. You are the special education organization that has primarily equipped me in the calling God has placed on my life.
- *Zeeland Christian School,* Zeeland, Michigan. You have allowed me to grow as a teacher and child of God in your community, my "home" away from home.
- *Zeeland Public Schools,* Zeeland. The partnership we have developed has allowed me to learn from your amazing staff.
- *Ottawa Area Intermediate School District,* Holland, Michigan. Carol Gray, Willie Wallis, and Mary Ann VanHousen, your consultants in the area of autism, have taught me so much over the years.
- *Lakeshore Vineyard Church,* Holland. You have allowed me to pilot many ideas, and you have honored, included, and loved me as an individual.
- *The Gray Center,* Kentwood, Michigan. You have given guidance and direction for this project. You are leaders in our community.
- *Dr. David Winstrom.* You have always encouraged me and have provided invaluable advice about the content and suggestions in this book.
- *Jan DeJonge.* Not only have you taught me so much, our friendship is a harbor in my busy days.
- *Pastor Jared Henderson.* You offered scriptural encouragement from Hebrews.
- *My friends and students on the autism spectrum.* Your names are too numerous to mention, but the experiences we have shared together have shaped my life.
- *David, Jetta, and Adam Winstrom; Leslie and Jessica Drahos; John DeCamp; Cathie and David Tien; Ryan Overweg;* and others who preferred to remain anonymous. You have been so willing to be interviewed for this resource book.
- *Mom and Dad, Mae and Andy Bandstra.* For decades, you've read my manuscripts and given cherished input.
- *My dear family, Barry, John, and James Newman.* Although sometimes my days are cluttered with many things, you are top on the list of my heart.
- *Jesus Christ.* You have changed my life forever! Your amazing revelation of how we are to live in community is the reason for this book.

—BJN

Contents

Everyone Welcome!

I am fairly certain that most churches have created a new staff position. Although many already have deacons, Sunday school teachers, and a host of other positions, my drive from home to work convinces me that many churches are now employing the services of a person responsible for one-liner signs. Signs like these are often the topic of conversation in our car:

- Know God, know peace. No God, no peace.
- God replies to knee-mail.
- Free trip to heaven—details inside.
- Best vitamin for a Christian? B1

One sign that many churches display is made up of only two words: *Everyone Welcome.*

Is it really possible that *everyone* is welcome at these churches? I drive by and imagine a long line of people at their doors: some people are in wheelchairs, others in business suits. Some have Down Syndrome, others walk while spinning a toy and rocking back and forth. Some people appear to have a lot of money, and others seem to have very little. The people in line display a rainbow of skin colors, abilities, and ages—but in my imagination, everyone is welcome.

In reality, it's likely that many persons with disabilities would not necessarily feel welcomed at these churches. Children with autism may not be included in Sunday school. Youth in wheelchairs may not be able to attend youth group functions for accessibility reasons. Parents presenting their precious child with special needs for baptism or dedication hear a pledge of support from the church, but that word is often not translated into action. Unsure how to handle such rejection, some parents take turns going to church while one parent stays home with the child. Some choose to have the entire family stay home. *"Everyone Welcome"* isn't meant for them.

I've observed that many persons with disabilities feel more support and inclusion from public schools and government agencies than they do from the body of Christ. At school the child is usually welcomed with open arms and tender loving care; adults are treated with dignity at work sites. A specialized program is designed for the child or adult, and a network of service providers ensures that each one's individual needs are met.

In contrast, the church may be a source of pain for many individuals with special needs. Most churches don't set out to exclude or isolate an individual. I've placed several phone calls to pastors and children's leaders on behalf of the children in my classroom. They are often eager to make some changes to allow families to worship together and offer appropriate support for children who may need something a bit specialized. In these situations, the problem was not a lack of acceptance—rather, the church simply didn't know what to do.

I believe that in order to be obedient to God's Word, the line at the church door must represent all kinds of people, including those with disabilities. *Everyone Welcome* is God's invitation, not ours. The acceptance, warmth, and sense of community that an individual feels on Sunday at church should make the Monday school or work experience pale in comparison. It is this vision that has prompted the writing of this book.

Although many resources are available in the area of ASD, very little is specific to equipping churches. It's my hope that God will use this resource to allow you and your church community to feel more confident in displaying and living out the invitation *Everyone Welcome.*

Introduction
Getting the Picture

Let's first take a look at the prevalence of ASD in our church communities. Then we'll outline how this resource is designed to help churches become welcoming places to those with ASD and also set some boundaries for using this resource.

Autism Spectrum Disorders (ASD) in the Church Community

How many people attend your church on a given Sunday? If 166 people attend, chances are great that *one* of those individuals has an Autism Spectrum Disorder. If your church has 500 people in attendance, divide that number by 166 to come up with the number of persons in your church family who likely fall on that spectrum. And don't forget to count those in your community involved in outreach programs your church offers. Currently, an estimated one person out of every 166 people falls somewhere on the autism spectrum. That number alone should make us realize that a church community that welcomes everyone will need to become familiar with strategies and ideas for including persons with ASD.

In reviewing a variety of church attendance statistics, it's obvious that persons with disabilities are vastly underrepresented in our congregations. I believe that God desires to use us to change these statistics. Jesus gave us numerous examples when he reached out to a person with seizures, to a person who was blind, to those unable to speak or hear, to those who were sick or lonely, and to the friends who walked with him each day. Jesus concluded his parable of the lost sheep with these words: "In the same way your Father in heaven is not willing that any of these little ones should be lost" (Matt. 18:14).

I've seen this parable lived out in totally contrasting ways in the lives of two friends with ASD. One family whose young son had autism was asked by an elder to leave him at home. Even though the rest of the family was welcome, the *one* was not. The family left this church and never went back. In my own church, a man diagnosed with Asperger Syndrome is a faithful friend and coworker in children's ministry. He fills his leadership role with great insight, impeccable attendance, and outstanding care for those who work under him. Knowing that he has Asperger Syndrome allows him to realize that at times he might need to ask about a social judgment call he must make. He handles that with wisdom, humility, and even humor.

Although Autism Spectrum Disorders will be defined in detail in section 2, an introductory definition is in order here. ASD includes Rett's Disorder, Autistic Disorder, Childhood Disintegrative Disorder, Asperger Disorder (also known as Asperger Syndrome), and Pervasive Developmental Disorder-Not Otherwise Specified (PDD-NOS). Children and adults with ASD exhibit a wide spectrum of differences in language understanding, social skills, repetitive themes and behaviors, perspective-taking ability, and sensory responses. These differences will be discussed in section 3.

This book has been written to help your church become that kind of welcoming and enfolding place. Join me for a quick overview.

This is not necessarily a book for those well-versed in special education or psychology. Its intent is to equip church leaders and members to better understand ASD and to select strategies that allow each individual to grow in Christ and to be more fully included within your church body.

We will begin by looking together at God's handiwork (section 1). Using my mother's knitting as an analogy, we'll reflect on the words of Psalm 139:13-14:

> For you created my inmost being; you knit me together in my mother's womb. I praise you because I am fearfully and wonderfully made.

In section 2, we'll explore Autism Spectrum Disorders in detail. We'll emphasize that labels and phrases we use to describe persons on the spectrum are only helpful when they allow us to better understand and support a child or an adult who is part of our faith community.

In section 3, we'll discuss five common areas of difference characteristic of people with ASD. We'll learn to appreciate how this wide spectrum of differences makes each person unique in God's family.

Section 4 describes ten strategies I've found helpful when working with people with ASD. We'll look at how these strategies can be applied with people of various ages and in a variety of situations and encourage you to use those that work in your specific setting.

Section 5 will equip your church to develop a long-range action plan as you strive to more fully include persons with ASD in the life of your church family. Suggestions will be given for forming a planning team, selecting a coordinator of special needs ministry, and for developing a *spiritual* IEP (Individual Education Program).

The reproducible resources include forms and other information referred to in sections 1-5. Sample forms will help you gather information about the children and adults in your church family with ASD. Job descriptions and other information will help you plan and carry out your ministry more effectively.

Before You Use This Resource

Before you begin reading and using this resource book, I want to share what you can—and cannot—expect from it.

- **This book is only the beginning to better understanding individuals with ASD.**

    I will propose general trends and ideas that have worked with many individuals, but these trends and ideas won't substitute for the task you have of knowing, understanding, and appreciating this unique person God created and brought into your body of believers.

- **This book is not intended to be a diagnostic tool.**

  Only psychologists, psychiatrists, or a school educational team are truly equipped to make a diagnosis of ASD. The information may make you think of a child or an adult that you know. Although God may guide you to encourage a child's parents or an adult to seek a professional assessment, this must always be done with extreme caution and must be couched in love, humility, patience, and prayer. Share only what you have observed, and avoid discussing your suspicions concerning the nature of the individual's condition.

- **The strategies listed in this book are helpful for many people, including those who do not have ASD.**

  You do not need to wait for a clinical label before using helpful strategies. For example, one strategy describes writing stories for children before they attend a Sunday school class. I use this strategy for all of the children in our church under the age of ten before we switch to summer programming. Parents and children each take a small booklet home with them to read before we switch to a new method of doing children's ministry during the summer months. That way, children can practice and understand what different routines will be in place before that first summer Sunday. Of the one hundred children age ten and under in our church, one child has autism and one child has Asperger Syndrome. The booklets are a great help for all of the children.

- **Numbers and names change over time.**

  To the best of my knowledge, the facts, figures, and labels included in this book are correct based on information currently available. Although I pray that this resource will be helpful for years to come, God gives new insights to researchers that will only enhance how we interact with one another.

- **Given the great number of people who have ASD, many treatment options are available.**

  It does not seem appropriate for a church to put together a large behavior program designed to teach a child more language skills. It does not seem appropriate to become a clinical treatment center. We as members of Christ's body are called to include and honor each person in the body. A church is called to touch each person with the love of Jesus, to nurture that individual in his or her relationship with Christ, and to offer opportunities to serve and grow in him. The strategies I suggest will be based on how we can best understand, communicate, and relate to one another.

- **No one strategy included in this book will work with every individual or in every situation.**

When I observe a child in a classroom setting, I often leave ten to fifteen ideas for a teacher to try. I am pleased when two or three of these strategies are effective and helpful. This book is filled with many suggestions, but your knowledge of the individual, God's guiding Spirit, and trial and error will help you locate the nuggets that are most beneficial for the individual in your community. Choose two or three strategies to try. If they are helpful, keep on using them. If not, replace them with another two or three. Work until you have the right package for the individual involved.

Whether your church already includes persons on the autism spectrum or you want to prepare for the time when they do, it's my prayer that the information and strategies in this book will guide and equip you. An incredible opportunity is waiting for you!

Section 1
God's Handiwork

God's Knitting: An Analogy

My mother knits. Although Mom did not pass on any knitting genes to me, she has a lifetime collection of afghans, baby blankets, sweaters, shawls, mittens, slippers, and vests credited to her amazing knitting talent. Some of the things she made for me when I was a child are so strikingly beautiful that I keep them in my closet today.

God knits too. Psalm 139:13-14 says: "For you created my inmost being; you knit me together in my mother's womb." God's end project is not a blanket or a sweater—God knits people.

I've noticed a number of striking similarities between my mother's knitting and God's knitting. Let's look at each one briefly.

Made in God's Image

My mother spends so much time with her projects, altering patterns and choosing colors and stitches, that it's easy to see that part of her is knitted into each garment. She is clearly visible in her projects.

The creation account in Genesis describes this same process. "So God created man in his own image, in the image of God he created him; male and female he created them" (1:27). When God creates our "inmost being" and knits us together, God himself is reflected in each one of us. As amazing as this is, when we become God's children through faith in Jesus Christ, that likeness becomes even clearer. The apostle Paul says, "And we, who with unveiled faces all reflect the Lord's glory, are being transformed into his likeness with ever-increasing glory, which comes from the Lord, who is the Spirit" (2 Cor. 3:18).

Made for a Purpose

The items my mother knits all have a different purpose. The colorful afghans she makes as a graduation gift for each of her grandchildren are very different from the small white blanket each one received as a newborn. The purpose and use of each item differs depending on how it is made.

God also has a specific purpose for each one of us. "For we are God's workmanship, created in Christ Jesus to do good works, which God prepared in advance for us to do" (Eph. 2:10). Paul offers this affirmation: "We have different gifts, according to the grace given us" (Rom. 12:6), and then challenges us to use these different gifts in proportion to our faith.

Made to Be Part of a Whole

My mother never intends for one item she's knitted to cover all of the clothing needs we have. Some items were made for warmer weather while others are for cold weather. Some items are to be used in a rugged setting while others require a delicate touch. Each is part of a larger wardrobe.

So too God created each one of his children to be part of a larger body of people. "Just as each of us has one body with many members, and these members do not all have the same function, so in Christ we who are many form one body, and each member belongs to all the others" (Rom. 12:4-5).

Clearly we were created to live in community, enjoying one another's gifts and ministering to one another's needs. Our strengths are knitted together for us to support others. Our weaknesses and needs are part of God's design so that others may minister to us. We truly were created to need one another.

"Fearfully and Wonderfully Made"
This understanding of God's knitting process certainly helps us to see our friends with special needs in a new light. Each of us, whatever our gifts and needs, our strengths and weaknesses, can say, "I praise you because I am fearfully and wonderfully made; your works are wonderful, I know that full well" (Ps. 139:14).

When the apostle Paul repeatedly asked God to remove his weakness, God said, "My grace is sufficient for you, for my power is made perfect in weakness" (12:9). Testifying to the reliability of God's grace, Paul says,

> Therefore I will boast all the more gladly about my
> weaknesses, so that Christ's power may rest on me.
> That is why, for Christ's sake, I delight in weaknesses,
> in insults, in hardships, in persecutions, in difficulties.
> For when I am weak, then I am strong (vv. 9-10).

Not only does God use our strengths and weaknesses, but God gives us these very explicit instructions as to how we should treat one another within his family:

> The eye cannot say to the hand, "I don't need you!" And
> the head cannot say to the feet, "I don't need you!" On
> the contrary, those parts of the body that seem to be
> weaker are indispensable, and the parts that we think
> are less honorable we treat with special honor. And the
> parts that are unpresentable are treated with special
> modesty, while our presentable parts need no special
> treatment. But God has combined the members of the
> body and has given greater honor to the parts that
> lacked it, so that there should be no division in the body,
> but that its parts should have equal concern for each
> other. If one part suffers, every part suffers with it; if
> one part is honored, every part rejoices with it.
>
> —1 Corinthians 12:21-26

The Bible completely affirms the worth and value of each individual as created by God. The only special arrangements God seems to make for persons with disabilities is qualifying them for a place of honor and special treatment within the body of Christ. Any church caught saying "I don't need you" to one of these individuals has completely violated and ignored God's instructions to the church. In contrast, individuals and churches testify to God's blessing as they purposefully embrace and include persons with special needs.

Ryan and Friends

Ryan is a great friend of my two sons. Ryan loves horses, chips and cheese, lightsabers, movies, and playing. He also happens to have Down Syndrome. John and Jim don't really pay much attention to his different facial features or difficult speech. They really enjoy his company and great personality. Although they coach Ryan's speech from time to time, the boys usually just have fun together.

It would be easy for someone to put a hand on the shoulders of my children and say, "How good of you to be nice to Ryan." It would appear to some that my boys are the "givers" and Ryan is the "taker." In God's body system, this is simply not the way it works. My boys have the gift of friendship and caring to offer Ryan, but Ryan also gives something to my children. His mother tells us that our whole family has made Ryan's "list." Every night, without fail, for the last six years, Ryan has prayed for each one of us by name. Imagine what a gift Ryan is giving to my boys and to our family!

Seeing People Through God's Eyes

Often insightful, one of my sons called me to the place where he does his best thinking. Soaking in the bathtub, he was troubled that he was unable to see God's amazing handiwork in a certain person. "Mom, I want to like this person, but he is so *annoying!*" As "Mrs. Special Education," I was supposed to have an answer. I had to admit that, seen through human eyes, this individual is annoying. But in that moment God showed me something important. I said to my son, "You're right. Most people would say that he is annoying. But if you can see something different in him, I will know that you are using God's eyes." I left the bathroom realizing that my own vision had just been adjusted. When my son called me back and said that he wanted to have this person over to our home, I knew that the Spirit was challenging him to take a closer look, to spend time finding what God had wrapped up in this child.

Jessica's Insight

At a conference I attended, the speaker was a brilliant individual with autism. At the close of the speech, a parent asked this question: "I want my child to know God. What can I do?" The speaker thought for a moment and then responded, "God is too hard for people with autism to understand. Next question." The instant pain on the mother's face brought tears to my eyes. I tried to make my way over to her, because I wanted to share a very different answer with her.

My friend Jessica is a Christian equipped with a passion for evangelism. Jessica loves to talk about her relationship with Jesus, and she cannot bear to think that some people in her life will not be with her in heaven.

God has given Jessica many insights, but I found one completely profound. Jessica described herself to her mother like this: "My body has autism, but my spirit does not." Jessica knows that her connection with God is not hindered by autism. From my observation, Jessica's connection with God is vibrant and all-pervasive in her life.

Jessica's comment made me think of the time when God sent Samuel to choose a king to replace Saul. Samuel was sure that God would choose Jesse's oldest son, but God said, "The Lord does not look at the things man looks at. Man looks at the outward appearance, but the Lord looks at the heart." Samuel had to look through God's eyes to see David—not as a young shepherd but as an individual God would use mightily in the days to come.

Jessica has given me this answer for the mother who asked the question at the conference:

> God made your daughter. Your child's heart is fully wired to
> be connected with God. God now reaches out through

Jesus to your daughter. When she receives Jesus as her Savior, that connection won't be weaker because of autism. Becoming a Christian won't take away her autism. But loving Jesus will give her the chance to serve God with all her heart, soul, mind, and strength. God will take who she is and fill her with his Holy Spirit to serve him and touch others around her.

As we talk more about Autism Spectrum Disorders, you will note that persons on this spectrum often have an intense area of interest that preoccupies a lot of mind space and time. Some people note the difficulty this can make in accomplishing tasks. I suppose that's one way of looking at it. True, it's a repetitive behavior—sometimes referred to as a *perseverative* behavior—but looking through God's eyes, we may gain a different perspective.

As we look more deeply into the topic of Autism Spectrum Disorders, we will discuss labels, diagnoses, differences, and more. This information will be helpful in interpreting terms used by parents, caregivers, or individuals with ASD.

Nuisance or Awesome Creature?

One of my young friends at Zeeland Christian School has been diagnosed with Asperger Syndrome. She absolutely adores animals. She wants to study them, read books about them, and talk about them. From bugs to larger critters, her curiosity is insatiable. Sometimes that love of animals prevents her from participating in the school day.

Attempting to use God's eyes, I see a different picture. It's possible that God is tired of us rushing past his amazing creation on our way to work or school, on our way to be "productive." The moth with delicate wings stuck to our windshield is one of his creations. While most of us will likely turn on the wipers to rid our vision of the obstruction, my friend will have a closer look.

Perhaps God allows my friend with Asperger Syndrome to delight more in his creation and pass on that sense of awe to those of us fortunate enough to be hanging next to her in God's closet. While my friend needs the advice and counsel of others to do well at school and home, I also need her in my life. Asperger Syndrome does not hinder her connection with God; it may even enhance it.

Our Response to God's Handiwork

Imagine my mother having spent weeks of time and energy on one of her knitting projects only to hear me express distaste for her precious gift:

- "I'd never wear a sweater like this!"
- "What a dumb-looking blanket. I'm not taking this anywhere."
- "These mittens are too uncomfortable. Give them to someone else."
- "I only like sweaters just like all the other ones in my closet. Don't give me something different."
- "Ugly, weird—no way. Just don't give me anything."

What is the likelihood that I would hurt my mother's feelings? What is the likelihood that I would ever get another knitted gift from her?

All too often, our reaction to people who have special needs is similar to those I'd never think of saying to my mother. We may be too uncomfortable even to give eye contact to an individual with special needs. We may see only the disability and not the person's gifts. We may focus only on the outward appearance and be unable to see the person's heart.

Using a previous example, you could view our friend Ryan only as a person with Down Syndrome—end of story. What a sad thing that would be! Ryan has a complex personality with loves and interests. Ryan is gifted by God to be an intercessor. He is not Down Syndrome Ryan. He is Ryan, my brother in Christ, who happens to have Down Syndrome as one of the many qualities that make him unique.

As a church community, we must not allow fear or uncertainty to rob us of enjoying and delighting in God's gifts to our community. By excluding those in the body of Christ who have a disability, we cheat our faith communities out of some of God's gifts for us. By including persons with special needs, we become a stronger body of believers.

The Gift of Adam

Adam's parents are quick to note how many people are thankful for his presence in their church community. Adam's heart is quickly displayed in his care for others.

The day Adam's pastor started crying as he made a difficult announcement, no one knew how to respond—except Adam. He broke the socially acceptable "rules of order" with his own tears as he hurried forward to give the pastor a hug. God used Adam to bring comfort in his own unique way.

Adam is a gift to that body of believers. Adam, who happens to have autism and Down Syndrome, makes that body stronger because of his presence. "Now to each one the manifestation of the Spirit is given for the common good" (1 Cor. 12:7).

May God equip you with his eyes. May God give you delight and joy as you see each individual as a gift from him, packaged with unique strengths and needs, designed to serve in your faith community. "Now you are the body of Christ, and each one of you is a part of it" (1 Cor. 12:27).

If you're taking the lead in welcoming people with ASD into your church, you'll want to help your entire church family learn along with you. In the reproducible pages at the back of this book, you'll find a summary called "I Belong" (p. 106). You may want to share this information in small group meetings, with your church council, in your church newsletter, and so on, in order to open the way for thoughtful discussion.

Autism Spectrum Disorders (ASD)

This summer my family vacationed in Michigan's Upper Peninsula. Knowing that gives you some idea of what we might have seen in the UP, but you'll know much more if I give you details about the towns we were in, where we stayed, and what we saw on our sightseeing trips.

Learning about Autism Spectrum Disorders is no different. The labels frequently used will give you some general idea about a person, but they really tell you very little about the specifics. Even though the words are large and the initials are many, it seems important to look at the labels and their meanings.

Our purpose in taking a closer look at ASD labels is not to give you a college-level understanding but rather to equip you to interact more easily with parents, individuals, and professional staff. Remember that knowing an individual's label will only get you as far as the UP. The best understanding will come when you get to learn more specifically about that individual's gifts and needs.

Putting Labels in Perspective

Although I don't want to minimize the helpfulness of a word or label, it's important to keep these descriptors in perspective. For example, my mother-in-law was diagnosed with diabetes. It's helpful for me to know this when she comes to my home. It helps me understand why we have needles in the garbage. It helps me stock up on the right kind of foods before she arrives for a visit. It also helped me understand the day she felt so strange in the grocery store and asked me to give her some orange juice before I had even paid for it. But it would be a mistake to overly focus on my mother-in-law's condition and fail to appreciate her unique personality and interests. We don't think about diabetes all the time; we laugh, talk, cry, shop, and watch movies together. Although I am grateful to be aware of the diabetic piece of my mother-in-law, it is only a portion of the complex and delightful person she is.

In the same way, the labels and phrases we use to describe persons with Autism Spectrum Disorders are only helpful when they allow us to better understand and serve these members of God's family. The label should not in any way take away from the fact that this is a complex person with individual gifts and needs. A label may describe certain features, but it describes only a fraction of who that person is in the body of Christ.

As you learn about labels used for individuals with ASD, please remember that it's the person first, then the label. I do not have a

diabetic mother-in-law; she is a person who also happens to have diabetes. I do not have autistic students and friends; I have students and friends who happen to have autism.

Understanding Autism Spectrum Disorders (ASD)

To best understand Autism Spectrum Disorders, it helps to picture ASD as an umbrella. *Pervasive Developmental Disorders (PDD)* is the term used by the American Psychiatric Association to categorize the five disorders identified below.

Autism Spectrum Disorders
Pervasive Developmental Disorders (PDD)

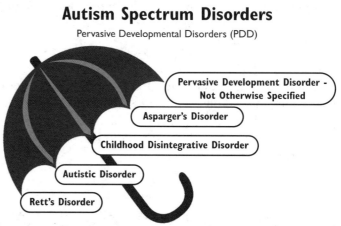

Pervasive Development Disorder - Not Otherwise Specified

Asparger's Disorder

Childhood Disintegrative Disorder

Autistic Disorder

Rett's Disorder

PDD is not in itself a disorder but simply a term that links the five disorders together into a category. As indicated in the illustration, Rett's Disorder, Childhood Disintegrative Disorder, Autism Disorder, Asperger Disorder, and Pervasive Developmental Disorder-Not Otherwise Specified (PDD-NOS) are categorized together because of the similarities that exist between them. If a person says, "I have PDD," that individual has one of the five disorders identified on the spokes of the umbrella. We'll define each of these in more detail in this section.

Rett's Disorder

Rett's Disorder, also called *Rett's Syndrome, Rett Syndrome,* or *Rett's,* is named after the doctor who observed certain characteristics in individuals. Although it is listed under the ASD category, some say that this disorder is different from the others in this category.

Recently scientists have discovered the gene responsible for Rett's Disorder. First thought to occur only in females, doctors now also see the genetic difference in some males who died before birth. People with Rett's Disorder develop according to typical patterns during the first five to eighteen months of life. Then things start to change. The child's head circumference begins to shrink. Social, motor, language, and cognitive skills that the child had acquired degenerate. The child develops unique hand movements: she may wring her hands, wash them over and over, or put them in her mouth.

The umbrella illustration organizes terms currently used in the *Diagnostic and Statistical Manual of Mental Disorders, Fourth Edition (DSM-IV),* published by the American Psychiatric Association. Many professionals in the field have been using the term *Autism Spectrum Disorders (ASD)* in place of *Pervasive Developmental Disorders (PDD).* Because it is prevalent in the literature, on websites, and in everyday conversation, I generally use the term Autism Spectrum Disorders (ASD) throughout this book (see "Using the ASD Label" on p. 28).

It's important to understand that a child who has Rett's Disorder will experience delays in many areas. Although some social skills and language abilities may rebound as the child learns and grows, this individual will most likely need a lifetime of care.

Sisters

I gained the most insight into Rett's Disorder from one of my fellow teachers whose sister Barb has this disorder. From my reading, I pictured a very limited individual. What I didn't picture was the amazing impact Barb has had on the life of my colleague.

My friend's eyes light up every time she mentions "Barbie." Through God's powerful direction, Barb had influenced her to choose a career in special education. Even though Barb lives in an adult care facility, she enjoys being together with my friend and her husband at their home. The tight sister bond between them was obvious when they walked into the teacher's lounge together one day. Unhindered by the issues related to Rett's, they enjoy being part of the same family.

I hope we can have that kind of relationship with others with this disorder who may enter our lives. We are all part of God's family—sisters and brothers in Christ.

Autistic Disorder

Autistic Disorder can also be called *Autism, Autistic Impaired,* or *AI.* Hearing these terms, we might visualize a person rocking, not communicating with others, or having great difficulty with social interactions. It's important to realize that the level of severity in autism varies greatly from individual to individual. In fact, one of your coworkers may have a diagnosis of high-functioning autism without you being aware of any symptoms.

A person is given an Autistic Disorder label when there are difficulties in three areas:

- social interaction and understanding
- language skills
- repetitive behaviors or interests

The next chapter will cover these areas in detail.

These three differences must be evident before the age of three. In fact, some evaluators ask parents for a videotape of their child's first birthday party. Often, many clues hidden in that party scene allow a trained eye to see these three traits at an early age. A person with autism may have a lower IQ score or a score that falls in the genius IQ area. Although the individuals with autism are diverse, these three threads of difference are evident in each person's life.

Happy Birthday!

One of the most spiritually life-changing experiences I have ever had was witnessing a child with autism giving her life to Jesus. Although I have seen it with others, this child had been under amazing spiritual attack. I now understand the strong Christian witness this girl would be and why Satan would have wanted to keep her silent.

Unhindered by the typical social veils we often wear and without access to the many religious phrases we use, Jessica's life transformed in one moment on February 29. She went from being sullen, unhappy, and unable to talk about Jesus to an instantly changed person the minute she prayed to become a Christian. She told everyone she met that day about her love for Jesus. She boldly asked others if they were Christians and gave them an invitation to join her. Her weak verbal skills were instantly enhanced by the power of the Holy Spirit.

But it's Jessica's face I remember the most. It was alive in a way I had never seen prior to her conversion. It dawned on me that conversion is like this for each of us, but often we suppress what is happening inside us for the sake of social convention. Jessica was (and still is) free of that. I still delight in looking at her face; I still praise God for changing her and for changing me.

Happy spiritual birthday, Jessica!

Childhood Disintegrative Disorder

Once a child has come through the early years, *Childhood Disintegrative Disorder* looks very similar to Autistic Disorder. The major difference happens in early childhood. Children with this condition are born and progress typically. They may develop great language, social, and motor ability, and even be potty trained. Then, somewhere between the ages of two and ten, they regress in at least two of these areas. All of a sudden, they are no longer able to use the bathroom or are unable to use and understand language as well as they did. These children also display the three traits evident with autism: difficulties with social skills and language skills, and repetitive behaviors or interests.

"Yes, I Love Jesus"

I have only had the opportunity to work with one child who has CDD. He was part of a choir I directed for persons with disabilities. Long before the time of inclusive education in Christian schools, Bob was part of the choir at Christian Learning Center (now CLC Network). We traveled to church services once a month and sang as a reminder to others of the giftedness of each member of the body of Christ.

Bob had a short solo in one of the songs. I sang to him: "Hey, Bob, do you love Jesus?" And he responded, "Yes, I love Jesus." I sang, "Are you sure you love Jesus?" Bob sang, "Yes, I'm sure I love Jesus." I sang, "Tell me, why do you love Jesus?" Bob replied, "This is why I love Jesus—because he first loved me."

Bob, one of the few members of that choir who could sing on key, witnessed to thousands of people over a ten-year period. The message that came from his mouth was a reminder that it's not what we do or know that allows us to have a relationship with Jesus. It's not our intellect or fluent verbal ability. God reaches his hand out to us in Jesus, and we get to take that hand. Bob was a powerful witness to that truth.

Asperger Disorder

Asperger Disorder is also known as *Asperger Syndrome* or *AS.* In the 1940s, Austrian physician Hans Asperger described people who seemed similar to persons with autism, but with distinct differences. When his work was translated into English in the 1990s, the diagnosis became prevalent.

To be diagnosed with Asperger Disorder, an individual must show difficulty with social interaction as well as exhibit some type of repetitive interest or behavior (two of the three characteristics of Autistic Disorder described on p. 24). The person must have an IQ in the average or above average range and will likely score well on speech and language tests. Because language and communication involve so many social skills, these scores can be misleading. One's vocabulary can be great while the ability to have a conversation can be difficult.

Most Likely to Be President

My oldest son John has a friend who has Asperger Syndrome. He is one of the smartest students in their eighth grade class. His name in the yearbook was accompanied with the caption "Most likely to be president one day."

My son and this boy share a love for classic rock music, and they often hang out together. John understands the characteristics that make his friend unique. He often goes to bat for him when teachers forget the difficulty he has with working in small groups. This friend is loyal, thoughtful, brilliant, musical, and a committed Christian young man.

I praise God for this friendship where each one sees the other as a gift from God. I see it as a model for the welcoming church.

Pervasive Developmental Disorder-Not Otherwise Specified (PDD-NOS)

Individuals with the *PDD-NOS* label show some signs of the other disorders in this category, but they don't fit exactly based on the criteria listed. For example, a person may have limited social understanding and language skills but show no evidence of a repetitive theme or behavior. That individual wouldn't qualify for another specific category, but the label PDD-NOS may help others understand him or her.

Community: BOC

What draw does Michigan have over California? It's probably not the gloomy winters!

Parents of a child diagnosed with PDD-NOS were looking for a Christian school that was willing to accept their son. Even though he was bright, was interested in learning, and had excellent language skills, staff at the school he was attending in California were not able to see past the label PDD-NOS.

This boy's parents wanted a community that would use and develop his gifts and support him in the areas that were difficult for him. They wanted him to belong. They found this community in Zeeland, Michigan. Linked with CLC Network in Grand Rapids, Michigan, the staff at Zeeland Christian School knows the value of creating a community where each child can belong. When you put all of the letters, labels, and children together, what you see through God's eyes is the body of Christ (BOC).

Using the ASD Label

So why use the term *Autism Spectrum Disorders* rather than *Pervasive Developmental Disorders?* First, it's helpful to know that a *spectrum* disorder indicates a range of behaviors and needs. A person with ASD can be impacted severely by the three differences. For example, a person may be unable to speak, prefer little social contact, and be consumed with lining up toys or cars—unable to break out of that routine. On the other hand, a person may have a more mild display of these differences: he may be confused by words with multiple meanings, make social errors or blunders when interacting, and be excited when talking about computers or trains.

Second, it is not our job to place people into one category or another. Diagnosis should be left to the professionals. Although it may be helpful to know specific words and labels, we do not need a label to welcome people with ASD into our church communities.

Finally, many helpful ideas and strategies offered in this resource book seem to benefit individuals in all of the categories. Rarely do I attend a conference and hear someone say, "You should do this *only* with children who have Asperger Disorder and not with a child who has PDD-NOS." Presenters usually give ideas that can be tried with anyone on the spectrum.

Multiple Special Needs

Many times a person diagnosed with Autism Disorder will only exhibit exceptional need in that one area. Sometimes a person may have Autism Disorder as well as Down Syndrome. An individual may have Asperger Disorder and also have cerebral palsy. A person with PDD-NOS may also be diagnosed with Attention Deficit Disorder.

This multiple diagnosis is not uncommon. I recently attended an Individual Education Program (IEP) meeting where a child qualified for three different areas of need. Once again, we need to emphasize that the specific diagnosis is not our major concern. The strategies listed in this resource book are often helpful for children and adults who may have more than one identified area of need.

Although the description of Autism Spectrum Disorders in this section is not exhaustive or technical, it is intended to make you more knowledgeable and understanding as you interact with individuals with ASD. When a label or diagnosis makes us more sensitive to an individual and her needs, it's helpful. When that same label obscures our vision and makes us see only the label and not an individual made in God's image with a unique package of gifts and needs, the label is a detriment. I pray that this knowledge will enable you to see people through God's eyes and more confidently welcome everyone into your church.

Section 3

Common Areas of Difference in Individuals with ASD

I am struck by the many differences God uses when equipping his people: "different kinds of gifts . . . , different kinds of service . . . , and different kinds of working" are embraced by "the same God [who] works all of them in all [people]" (1 Cor. 12:4).

Although differences can sometimes make us surprised or uncomfortable, they can also be a source of joy and wonder. Many times, people with ASD make unique contributions to our world and lives because of their differences. For example, a person focused on computers and technology can be of great help to those who barely know how to turn on the machine. An individual dedicated to making the numbers come out right at the end of the day can be invaluable as an accountant for those who find no delight in numbers.

In Aisle 9

A fifth grader with Asperger Disorder is enthralled with retail. He knows who is going into business and who is going out of business. When shopping, he has a store impeccably cataloged and knows what items are located in a specific aisle.

While shopping with his mother at Meijer, a regional chain store, this detail-oriented child immediately recognized a problem. Meijer had changed aisle numbers! Surprised to find out that his mom never looked at aisle numbers, he was incredibly helpful in navigating the newly organized store.

In this section, we'll look at some of the common areas of difference in persons who have ASD. The first three—language understanding, social skills, and repetitive themes and behavior—are all areas covered by an evaluator when making a specific diagnosis within the spectrum of disorders. Although not generally included in a formal evaluation, it's also worth noting differences in the areas of perspective-taking ability and sensory responses. In section 4, we'll look at strategies for dealing with these five common areas of difference and discover ways to grow together as the body of Christ.

Language Understanding

The word *language* covers a very large territory. Language skills allow us to understand words, follow directions, and express ourselves verbally in words and sentences. Combined with social skills, language helps us interact with others and carry on meaningful conversations.

The differences in language are evidenced in a variety of ways in individuals with ASD. A person more significantly impacted with this difference may be unable to speak. This individual may have been taught some sign language or may be unable to use this method of communication as well.

Many individuals with ASD develop a great vocabulary, but some struggle with grammar and putting sentences together correctly. One child I currently serve is just learning all of the amazing rules in reading the English language. We are adding *ed* to the ends of words to make them past tense. It's hard for this child to understand that we don't always follow this rule. "I *broked* the chair" makes more sense to him at this point than "I broke the chair." Correct pronouns and gender terms can also be difficult. Talking about a female, this student said, "He came to my house." Words like *Mr., Mrs., him, her, he,* and *she* often get confused in conversation or writing.

Although individuals with Asperger Disorder score very well on tests of language, you may find differences in conversation where language intersects with social skills. Eye contact may be difficult. Voice volume may be too loud or too soft. Many times the give and take of talking is very one-sided and focused on the interests of the person with Asperger Disorder. At times, an individual may say something hurtful to another person and be completely unaware that it was inappropriate. A person may deliver some sad news or comment about a serious situation with facial expression that does not match the words. Children often get into trouble when they smile while a teacher is reprimanding them. The teacher may interpret this as further disrespect instead of understanding that facial features don't always match the content of language.

Some individuals struggle with words and idioms that have multiple meanings. Many persons with ASD comprehend language very literally. For example, most people interpret the expression "Break a leg" as a kind gesture wishing someone good fortune. A person with ASD might wonder why we would want someone to break a bone.

Time Isn't Time

A good example of the struggle with multiple meanings happened in a classroom discussion about feeling sad and feeling happy. A group of four children was seated at the table. One of the children had autism; the other three struggled with speech and language issues. The child with autism has a very high IQ score, but because of his language differences, the discussion was difficult for him. "Tell me about something that makes you feel sad," the teacher said. After the other three children responded, the child with autism said, "When I hurt my knee." Then the teacher said, "Tell me a *time* you were happy." The other children responded well to this question, and then the boy with autism said, "About five o'clock." Based on the literal meaning of time, he answered the question correctly, but the other children were able to answer the question with specific examples of times they felt happy.

Our faith language is also filled with interesting phrases. Interpreted literally, these things can be scary and create confusion. Imagine literally being "covered with the blood of Jesus" or "giving your heart to Jesus."

By interpreting faith language for persons with ASD, I have been able to process more deeply many areas of the Christian faith. For example, a woman was unable to take communion because she thought the juice was literally the blood of Jesus. God showed me a deeper meaning to communion as I translated that phrase for her. When a student was very confused because *dead* meant always dead, I was challenged to describe the resurrection of Jesus in a way that stretched and delighted me. When we perceive we are the givers, it's God who is truly the giver.

Like the area of language understanding, *social skills* is a term that covers a wide field. Think about your day. What activities were done completely in isolation? If you are a member of a family, your home is filled with opportunities to interact with others. Your job or school is another place filled with social demands and interactions. Even activities like shopping, going to church, going to the bank, or enjoying time at the beach require interactions with others. Now imagine that interacting with others is not a strength you have.

Persons with ASD really struggle to figure out their social world. Based on studies, it's become clear that this difference originates in the brain. The portion of my brain that makes social decisions and judgments is very small and efficient. I can walk into a room and immediately sense the mood of others and how I should fit in. I can look at an individual's face and make a good guess as to how that person is feeling. I can say something to an individual and immediately know how my words registered and whether I should steer clear of that topic or continue talking. These social skills are very difficult for persons with ASD. The portion of their brain that makes social decisions is much larger and far less efficient.

Analyzing another person's face is very hard. Most of us focus on a person's eyes, while many people with ASD focus on a person's mouth. Although the mouth is used for speaking and thus would seem to be significant, the eyes are often the window to a person's feelings. It's hard for a person with ASD to walk into a room and make good guesses about what is going on. Is this a quiet place? Is this a serious place? People with ASD often are taught to analyze many features, and that takes more time. It's easier to memorize rules about certain places: a church is generally a place to be quiet, a store is generally a place to be louder. Most of the time, rules like these are helpful, but situations and conditions can change quickly.

These social differences often create two responses in persons with ASD. Some individuals prefer to pull away from social interactions. Physically, some desire more time to be alone. Conversationally, to help focus on your words, an individual may not make eye contact or try to analyze your facial expressions. Some children need recess to be a time when they can play alone and push the social "reset" button. The opposite response is to plow right into the middle of social situations. This courageous approach often results in social errors and blunders.

Knowing this information about another individual can really be helpful in interpreting social interactions. But more importantly, social interactions require more than one person—and *we* are that other person! We are the ones with excellent social skills. So it's far easier to change our side of the equation than it is to change the side of the individual with ASD. Many of the strategies suggested in this book count on us being the one to do some changing—not the person with ASD. Isn't it amazing that God can use the needs of others to bring about growth in our own lives?

Repetitive Themes and Behaviors

My classroom was never cleaner than when I had a boy with ASD who needed to have the toy shelf arranged a certain way before doing any of his work. My brain is also saturated with details about trains, Star Wars, and tigers. I know many movie lines from *Veggie Tales*. I have watched children play with cars, not driving them through the Fisher Price garage but lining them up in order of size or features. These are examples of repetitive themes and behaviors of individuals with ASD.

For some individuals, these issues are physical. A person may flap her hands or poke at her eyes when looking at the lights. For others, the issues often center on a favorite topic. These might include a particular animal or some type of movie. Some adults have chosen a profession that fits this area of interest. A university professor may leave no stone unturned in the field of geology. A computer expert may know every wire and connection inside that box. Many individuals with ASD have made significant contributions in an area of study because of this characteristic.

So why is this a problem? Many times this passion for a topic completely rules a person's thought life. It might be hard for an individual to talk about anything but computers or chess. It might be difficult to relate to others who don't know about a sloth or trains. It might be hard to engage in learning when the shelves are slightly messy.

This quality of persons with ASD has been a great source of delight for me. I have learned many things from my friends, and together we have figured out ways to move beyond their favorite topic into other areas. When God focuses an area of interest on things such as bringing others to Christ, or prayer, the effect can be powerful. As we look at strategies related to social skills in section 4, I can guarantee that you will enjoy many of your friend's areas of study and interest.

Perspective-Taking Ability

To better understand differences in the area of perspective-taking ability, try these exercises:

- Close your eyes. Can you describe the wall or scene that is directly behind you without looking at it?
- An individual carrying a tissue has tears coming down each cheek. As you meet, you remember reading in the obituary section of the newspaper that her father had just died. Can you imagine how she is feeling right now?
- As you are talking to someone in the church foyer, he waves to another person and turns his body at an angle away from you. What might you think about his actions?

All of these situations involve a complex task that we do many times each day. We can visualize something different than what our eyes can see. We are able to jump out of our own head, so to speak, and jump into the head of someone else. Although visual perspective is helpful, taking the perspective of another person allows us to know how to act with others in various situations. It allows us to guess what another person is thinking or feeling. As a speaker, I jump into the heads of people all the time. If they look bored or tired, I change the pace of what I am saying or insert an activity. If they look curious or confused, I may add more detail or explain it a different way.

Having good perspective-taking ability allows us to get embarrassed. In order to get embarrassed, we need to know what another person is thinking about us. It allows us to be good at lying, which is actually a high-level perspective-taking skill. To lie well, an individual must be able to know what another person might think about a situation and then change the story so that the other person will react more favorably to our actions or story. Middle school children have amazing perspective-taking ability—a skill we desperately need to navigate the social world. They not only seem to know who likes Tim, but they know what Mary thinks about what Sue thinks about Tim.

Think of one time today that you have used your perspective-taking ability. When you pray, do you make assumptions about individuals and how they may feel or what they are thinking? When you read the Bible, can you put yourself in the sandals of someone in the story and imagine yourself in that place? When Jesus turned over the tables of the money-changers in the temple, do you have accurate insight into his feelings?

Now imagine being unable to accurately predict the thoughts or feelings of another individual. Imagine being unable to accurately read a social or physical situation and then react accordingly. Persons with ASD have a very difficult time with this skill. That limits their ability to interpret situations, feelings, and interactions. Go back to the three tasks I asked you to complete at the beginning of this section. What if you were unable to complete these tasks? How might that alter your actions in those situations?

Just knowing this information can help us interpret the social interactions of individuals with ASD. We'll give specific strategies for strengthening their perspective-taking ability in section 4.

Sensory Responses

Most of us take our senses for granted. When I work in my office, I enjoy the birds in the trees outside, the morning sunshine streaming in my window, the taste and smell of coffee, and the cushioned office chair by my computer desk. When my children get up and turn on their music, I'll likely be more aware of my senses and scramble for the volume button.

Beyond the five senses we normally think about, we have other systems at work. I get feedback from my fingers when typing to know where my hands are without looking at them. As the muscles in my hands and body give me constant feedback, I know when to shift positions in my chair. Even without arms on the chair, I can maintain good balance, and I don't worry about falling over. These sensory systems, known as *vestibular* and *proprioceptive* systems, are also at work along with the others to keep my body aware of and reacting appropriately to my surroundings.

Different sounds, sights, smells, tastes, and feelings often interrupt our day. Most of the time, our bodies make calculations to compensate for those sensations, and we move on. Sometimes our bodies learn new skills so that these sensations are no longer an issue. I don't usually think about walking—except when I approach a moving sidewalk at an airport. Then I have to think about how to place my foot and how to time my steps. Many frequent flyers encounter this situation so often that their sensory systems have memorized how to do moving sidewalks along with regular ones.

Many people with ASD respond differently to sensory stimuli. A sound that is not loud to me may be truly painful for an individual with ASD. This person may cover her ears or avoid situations where sudden noises may occur. In contrast, another individual with ASD may not respond at all to sounds that most others hear. This can be true with any sense. A light touch for me may be painful to a friend with ASD. A smell barely noticed by one person may create a horrible environment for another.

In working with individuals who have ASD, I have found differences in the area of sensory response to be a key in setting up a comfortable environment. If a child is sensitive to noise, imagine riding a bus to school. If a person is hurt by light touch, imagine having to shake hands or give hugs during greeting time at church. Knowing about these differences can allow us to make appropriate changes in the environment.

Although we've identified five common areas of difference in children and adults with ASD, it's important to remember that each person is unique. No two individuals will experience these differences in exactly the same way or to the same degree—that's why we use the term *spectrum*. It's my prayer that by knowing about these common areas of difference, you will be equipped to select strategies that will work in a variety of situations. That's the purpose of the next section.

Section 4

Ten Strategies for Including Individuals with ASD

If given a choice, I prefer to stay in a five-star hotel. Although slightly more expensive, I know a hotel with a five-star rating will provide awesome accommodations. Staff will make sure that I have a good stay. They won't just "leave the light on"; they will put chocolates on my pillow, call me by name, and have a showerhead that makes me want to stay another night. They will not assume that each guest likes the same things. My particular needs and wants matter at a five-star hotel.

Jesus knew all about providing five-star experiences. While teaching crowds of people might seem more efficient, Jesus took time to meet individuals at their point of need. Consider these examples from the gospel accounts of Jesus' ministry:

- Zacchaeus needed some one-on-one time with Jesus, so Jesus invited himself to dinner (Luke 19:1-9).
- The children needed to know they belonged, so Jesus took them in his arms and blessed them (Mark 10:13-16).
- The disciples needed clearer understanding, so Jesus told a story about a farmer and compared the seed to the word of God (Luke 8:1-15).
- The sellers in the temple needed correction, so Jesus chased them out and set them straight (John 2:12-20).
- The woman caught in adultery needed forgiveness, so Jesus dared any of her accusers who were without sin to throw a stone at her (John 8:1-11).
- The crowd of 5,000 needed food, so Jesus took a little boy's lunch and fed them (Matt. 14:13-21).
- Thomas needed to see and touch to believe that Jesus was alive, so his Savior held out his nail-scarred hands (John 20:24-29).

Note the diversity in these examples. No person or group was like any other; no method Jesus used to reach them was just like any other. When we recognize and honor that diversity in the body of Christ, then our churches will be five-star churches.

So how does a five-star church interact with children and adults who have ASD? We begin, as we have in sections 1 through 3 of this resource book, by understanding that each person has a unique package of gifts and needs and is a part of the body of Christ. Then we match our actions to reflect what Scripture teaches us:

> God has arranged the parts in the body, every one of them, just as he wanted them to be. . . . The eye cannot say to the hand, "I don't need you!" And the head cannot

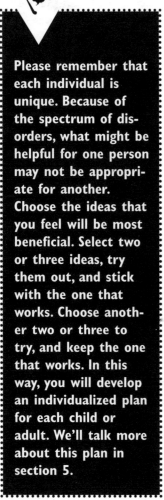

say to the feet, "I don't need you!" On the contrary, those parts of the body that seem to be weaker are indispensable, and the parts that we think are less honorable we treat with special honor. . . . God has combined the members of the body and has given greater honor to the parts that lacked it, so that there should be no division in the body, but that its parts should have equal concern for each other.

—1 Corinthians 12:18, 21-25

That's a tall order, but we can learn how to do it! In this section, I'll share ten strategies that have proved helpful when interacting with children and adults who have ASD. We'll look at how to

- gather information about the person with ASD.
- share information with others who need to know.
- monitor sensory input in our church environment.
- think alongside the person with ASD.
- make routines comfortable.
- use advance warning systems.
- close the communication gap.
- use visuals to reinforce what we say.
- write stories to help people with ASD anticipate new situations.
- teach instead of react.

For each strategy, you'll find

- a brief description.
- practical ideas for using the strategy in specific situations.
- sample forms and other helpful tools. (These will be referred to in this section and included in the reproducible resources section of this book.)

Please remember that each individual is unique. Because of the spectrum of disorders, what might be helpful for one person may not be appropriate for another. Choose the ideas that you feel will be most beneficial. Select two or three ideas, try them out, and stick with the one that works. Choose another two or three to try, and keep the one that works. In this way, you will develop an individualized plan for each child or adult. We'll talk more about this plan in section 5.

Strategy 1: Gathering Information About the Person with ASD

While knowing something about Autism Spectrum Disorders is the place to start, it's not the same as knowing something about a child or adult who happens to have ASD. You'll need more specific information before you can effectively welcome each person into your faith community.

But whom do you contact? Will everyone want to give you information? Although you will need to be sensitive to the Spirit's leading, you'll likely recognize these four categories of people:

- those you know are diagnosed with ASD because they have given you that information.
- those who have been diagnosed but have chosen not to share that information.
- those you suspect have ASD, given certain behaviors, but have not been diagnosed.
- those with ASD who are unable to tell you. (To protect the legal rights of clients, caregivers are not allowed to divulge this information.)

It's often easiest to start gathering information with some type of survey. This can be on your registration card for children's ministry. It can be part of a member or visitor survey, or it could be an invitation extended as part of a Sunday message. Whatever method you choose, start with those who have already shared that they have ASD. As other members of your congregation see that you handle this information in a trustworthy way, they may step forward as well. In order to reach some of these people, you might want to begin by giving an open invitation that focuses more on special needs rather than on ASD specifically.

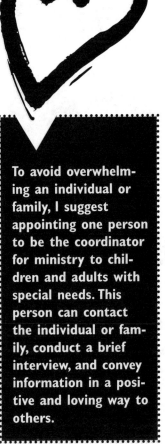

To avoid overwhelming an individual or family, I suggest appointing one person to be the coordinator for ministry to children and adults with special needs. This person can contact the individual or family, conduct a brief interview, and convey information in a positive and loving way to others.

Registration Cards for Children's Ministry

Consider making a registration card for anyone who sends a child in grade 12 and below to your church programs. In addition to requesting name, address, phone number, birthday, grade, and other important data, simply add the following: **Does your child have any special needs we should be aware of? This information will be shared only at your request, but it will allow us to better meet your child's individual needs.**

This gives parents a chance to write down special needs like peanut allergies, Attention Deficit Disorder, reading or writing challenges, autism, and so on.

To keep information current, ask parents to enroll their child each year. For example, a child may not be diagnosed with ASD until grade 3. If you only require people to fill out information one time, you would not get this updated form. You may also want to make it a routine practice to hand this card to each visitor who has children. Require that the card is filled out before a child is admitted to nursery, Sunday school, or any other children's ministry program.

Interview Questionnaires for Children's Ministry

Making the first personal contact is often the hardest part, but registration information is an excellent way to open the door to further conversation. You'll want to use an interview questionnaire to gather more specific information about a child's special needs.

Getting to Know Justin

A phone call to a parent might go something like this:

> Hi, Mrs. Gaines. This is Jody from Faith Church calling. I am the coordinator for ministry to children and adults who have special needs. We are so excited to have Justin as part of our children's ministry, and we want to make this a positive experience for him. You indicated on the registration card that your son has some special needs. I'd like to visit with you a few minutes to learn more about Justin. Is this a good time for you? [Be prepared to call at another time or to visit in person in your office or at the person's home.]

> I have a brief list of questions I'd like to ask. (See Sample Interview Questionnaire for Children's Ministry on p. 107; adapt as needed to fit each situation.)

> With your permission, I'd like to share a summary of this information with Justin's teachers. (The next strategy, described on pp. 49-57, will explain how to share information with others. You'll want to explain these procedures to the parent.)

Note that the interview questionnaire begins by asking about a child's strengths and interests. It's tempting to begin by asking for a child's diagnosis. Starting with an individual's gifts communicates clearly that you see this person as much more complex and diverse than one label describes.

Bulletin Announcements for Children's Ministry

Another way to advertise that you would like to better know the children in your congregation who have special needs would be in a weekly bulletin or announcement format. This gives important contact information to families who have a child with special needs, and it allows you to communicate that this is an important value for your faith community. You could say something along these lines:

> **If your child has any type of special need, please contact Jody, our coordinator for ministry to children and adults with special needs. We want to make children's ministry a positive experience for each child God brings to us.**

This reminder is especially relevant when working with young people who have multiple special needs, including ASD (see section 2, p. 28). If your church already has a Friendship program, it's important that the coordinator for ministry to children and adults with special needs works closely with the Friendship leader. To learn more about starting a Friendship program in your church, call Friendship Ministries at 1-888-866-8966 or visit the Friendship website at www.Friendship.org.

If parents or guardians respond to your announcement, let them know that your coordinator for ministry to children and adults with special needs will contact them sometime during the week. Or present the interview questions in written format so that parents can fill out the survey immediately (see Sample Interview Questionnaire for Children's Ministry, p. 107). Review the information and decide together with the parent what the teacher or group leader needs to know for that day; then arrange for the coordinator to follow up and discuss the survey in more detail.

Visits with Day School Teachers for School-age Children

Although each has a different mission, many similarities exist between church education programs and day schools. Both private and public school staff are generally eager to share information that will enhance a child's experience in worship and church education. The coordinator for ministry to children with special needs can contact a child's teacher and ask many of the same questions asked of parents (see Sample

Based on over twenty years of experience, Friendship Ministries, a program for youth and adults with cognitive impairments, affirms that

inclusion of people with cognitive impairments in the regular programs of the church is the ideal situation. A few adjustments may have to be made, but generally inclusion of children with cognitive impairments in the regular Sunday school class works very well. Realistically, inclusion often begins to fall apart around the time of adolescence, when social situations begin to vary dramatically. It's at this age that we recommend separate Friendship groups for people who have cognitive impairments, though we still advocate for their full inclusion in the life of the church.

Interview Questionnaire for Children's Ministry, p. 107). Teachers might share insights about the child in a more structured, formal setting. They may be willing to share techniques they've found helpful. In some cases, you may wish to visit the school to observe a child in this setting (see suggestions on p. 47).

Visits with teachers and to a child's school require *written* consent from the child's parent or guardian. Always respect this rule of confidentiality.

Congregational Survey for Adult Ministry

In order to identify adults who might appreciate some special understanding and care, you may wish to distribute a congregational survey. The survey could request common data such as name, address, phone, e-mail address, and areas in which an individual might like to serve. A question to determine special needs might be stated like this:

> **To help us meet the needs of each individual in our faith community, please list any special needs that may prevent you from participating fully in the life of our church. Jody, our coordinator for ministry to children and adults with special needs, will contact you to determine how we can best enable you to use the gifts God has given you.**

Recognize that surveying adults will not yield the same response rates as requiring registration for participation in children's ministry. Even so, it's a place to start, and the survey can provide an opening for follow-up contacts.

Interview Questionnaire for Adults

When people indicate a special need on a survey, be ready to contact them within a few days. When you gather sensitive information from a person, you will establish a trust relationship if you handle information confidentially and efficiently.

Getting to Know Lila

A follow-up phone call to an adult with special needs might go something like this:

> Good morning, Lila. This is Jody from Faith Church calling. I am the coordinator for ministry to children and adults with

special needs. We are glad to have you as part of our faith community, and we want to make this a great experience for you. You indicated on our recent congregational survey that you have some special needs. I'd like to visit with you for a few minutes to learn more about how we can help you. Is this a good time for you? [Be prepared to call at another time or to visit in person in your office or at the person's home.]

I have a brief list of questions I'd like to ask. (See Sample Interview Questionnaire for Adult Ministry on p. 109; adapt as needed to fit each situation.)

With your permission, I'd like to share a summary of this information with our congregational care committee. (The next strategy, described on pp. 49-57, will explain how to share information with others. You'll want to explain these procedures to Lila and be specific about who will receive the information.)

The sample conversation with Lila assumes that she may be new to your faith community. Obviously, you'll want to adapt your approach for someone who has been a part of your church for a long time but who may have more recently experienced a special need. Or you may need to confess that your faith community has been slow to respond to a need that has existed for some time.

Categorizing Pictures for Children and Adults

When an individual with ASD is unable and a trusted family member or friend is unavailable to complete an interview questionnaire, I keep paper and pencils close at hand. It's amazing what information can be gathered with a few simple stick-figure drawings.

Some adults with ASD prefer to answer questions in written form. Even answering questions in an e-mail format can be helpful. This takes the often confusing social dimension away and allows the individual to focus on communicating the information at a slower pace than over the phone or face to face. Some individuals with ASD or multiple needs may require the help of a trusted friend or family member to fill out the survey.

"I Like It/I Don't Like It"

Before I met with a young man I'll call Joe, I printed a collection of stick-figure drawings depicting aspects of church life that I had found on my computer. I also made some blank cards the same size. I drew a happy face in the top left corner of a sheet of paper and a sad face in the top right corner as illustrated below. I wrote "I like it" by the happy face and "I don't like it" by the sad face. I made a second sheet just like it.

As I began visiting with Joe, I explained that we were going to talk about things he likes (things that make him feel happy) and things he doesn't like (things that make him feel sad) about our church. Then I showed Joe one drawing at a time and asked him to place each under the happy or sad face. When all the stick-figure drawings were in place, I asked Joe if he wanted to add any other pictures. We used the blank cards to illustrate Joe's ideas.

Here's how Joe felt about our church:

Then I took the second sheet with happy and sad faces and moved the pictures Joe had placed under the "I don't like it" category to the new sheet. I said, "I see you don't like the singing time. What can we do to make singing time something you do like?" I drew an arrow from the picture on the "I don't like" side to a space on the "I like it" side. As Joe talked, I wrote down his comments on the arrows:

- If I knew when the organ was going to start playing, it wouldn't make me jump as much.

- The kids are all too loud!

That's helpful information to work with as we think about solutions.

As you categorize pictures, try not to sit directly across from an individual with ASD. It's most helpful to sit beside a person or beside and slightly behind. This allows both of you to concentrate on the task. Focusing on a picture together is far easier than having a face-to-face conversation.

Once you've identified things a person doesn't like, you're ready to brainstorm solutions. Additional strategies described in this section will give you a variety of ideas.

Observation of Children or Adults with ASD

You will encounter times when no information is available. Either the individual is not able to give input, a family or individual does not wish to share information, or the individual is part of the adult care system and confidentiality legally prevents caregivers from divulging anything to a church. In that case, you may want to use your own observation skills to gather information. You'll find a Sample Observation Form on page 111 in the reproducible resources section of this book.

The process of categorizing pictures I used with Joe is a useful technique to use as part of a learning environment as well. After teaching a lesson or giving a message, provide pictures or words of the main points of the lesson and let children or adults categorize them under the headings "I understand" and "I don't understand." Then present the more difficult concepts in a way that the individual can understand. You can use this same technique as a prayer tool when an individual is nonverbal. One heading could say "Thank you, Lord" and the other say, "I ask you, Lord." Provide pictures or words to sort, and let that guide how you pray with an individual. Once you try this, you will soon find many applications for this technique—in Sunday school, Friendship groups, small group Bible study, and so on.

When gathering information, we sometimes underestimate the amazing connection we have to God. Ask God for a glimpse of each person's gifts and needs. Let's not make prayer our last resort—go to the Creator first!

When an individual lives in an adult care facility, agencies have a legal responsibility to protect the privacy of residents. However, many are legally able to share important information if it is "in the best interest" of the client. You might want to form a relationship with the supervisor of the facility. Share your excitement and vision for how you hope to more fully include the individual with ASD, and pray that they will find it in the resident's best interest to share some important information with you.

The care facility can also provide a unique educational and service opportunity for the congregation. Some churches regularly check for needs in the group home, and then try to fill those through special offerings or donations. Sometimes homes are in need of companions who will come and bake cookies or have coffee with individuals. Sometimes they need a door widened for a wheelchair. Or a person who no longer has family around might need a new appliance or birthday gift. The outward display of Christ's love is a powerful witness to caregivers and residents as well.

Strategy 2: **Sharing Information with Others Who Need to Know**

"What you don't know won't hurt you." That may be true in some situations, but when working with children and adults who have ASD, it's important to know critical information.

Jesus was a master at giving critical information when people had a wrong impression. Ready to stone a woman caught in adultery, Jesus gives one piece of advice to her accusers: "If any one of you is without sin, let him be the first to throw a stone at her" (John 8:7). That one sentence allowed people to see the situation in a new light. One by one, they walked away.

When welcoming children and adults with special needs into our churches, I have found that this one strategy often makes the difference between accepting or rejecting a person. Accurate information, stated positively and honestly, is powerful. For example, it's helpful to know that a child has ASD and is sensitive to loud sounds. Thus, if the microphone malfunctions and squeals during worship and the child covers his ears and starts to scream, the parents are not blamed for poor behavior management, and the child is not labeled a problem child. Knowing that the child has experienced excruciating pain from this unexpected noise allows people to respond with compassion and understanding rather than judgment.

Who Needs to Know?

If sharing information about children and adults with ASD is critical, who needs that information? Three groups within the church can benefit from positive and honest information:

- Leaders. From pastors planning a worship service to the mentor assigned to a friend in the Friendship group to youth pastors working with teenagers, leaders need information in order to best plan and interact with those involved in the life of the church.
- Peers. Depending on the situation, an entire congregation, an adult small group, a child's Sunday school class, a Friendship group, or a youth group needs information to help them understand and accept an individual as a unique part of their group.
- Children and adults with ASD need information to help them succeed in the church environment.

This second strategy will focus on sharing critical information with leaders and peers. Other strategies will be geared to giving individuals with ASD the information they need to more fully participate in the life of the church.

Sharing critical information is the focus of the book *Helping Kids Include Kids with Disabilities* (Barbara J. Newman, © 2001, Faith Alive Christian Resources). Written to package many of the strategies I have learned in an inclusive private school environment, this book is an excellent resource for churches. It sets the ground work for positively interacting together in the body of Christ. One section deals with ASD; additional sections address other special needs. You can order this book at www.Friendship.org or www.faithaliveresources.org.

Broad Information About ASD for Leaders of Children and Adults

If your congregation includes an individual with ASD, you'll find this book helpful for equipping leaders. Place a copy in your church library and specifically target teachers and leaders who will teach or mentor a person with ASD.

You may wish to gather those most involved with the child or adult with ASD as a small group to discuss topics covered in this book. Begin with the first three sections, perhaps in three different sessions. You'll find that once leaders receive information and have a chance to share concerns, they'll feel more at ease.

Another possibility would be to invite a guest speaker to a leader training session. This allows time for leaders to receive broad information from an expert in the field of ASD and an opportunity for them to ask specific questions.

Specific Information About a Child with ASD for Children's Ministry Leaders

The coordinator for ministry to children and adults with special needs should contact the family of the individual for more specific information. Coordinators may use the sample interview questionnaire (see p. 107) as the basis for developing a profile that can be shared with Sunday school teachers, Friendship leaders, and mentors, youth pastors, and other church leaders who work with a child with ASD.

When preparing a profile of a child with ASD, keep the following tips in mind:

- Begin by describing the child's interests and gifts.
- Emphasize that the child's diagnosis is only one part of the individual.
- State information positively and honestly.
- Limit the profile to one page so leaders can process the information quickly.
- Include the names of resource people who can help serve this child.
- Share a copy of the profile with parents and get their *written* permission to share it with leaders.
- If parents are not happy with your draft, allow them to rewrite or reword the profile so that they will be comfortable sharing it with leaders.
- If appropriate, and if suggested by parents, show a copy to the child. If stated positively and honestly, the profile will honor and affirm the individual.

Although a profile may be formatted any way you wish, the sample on pages 51-52 shows one way to take information from the interview questionnaire and put it into a profile format. The final section of this book includes a form suggesting specific strategies leaders can try, which can be attached to the profile.

Presenting David

Profile written by Jody Kobes, coordinator of ministry to children and adults with special needs

Date: September 5, 2005

This profile is confidential information. David's parents have given permission to share this with you to help you create a place for David to grow in Christ.

Programs David will attend this year: Sunday school (grade 1), junior choir, and children's worship.

Interests and joys: David enjoys reading, Game Boy, videos, puzzles, matching and memory games, and music. David's visual abilities (solving problems with his eyes and understanding visual concepts) are far beyond his years, probably far exceeding your ability or mine in this area. Academically, David understands and knows at least as much if not more than others his age.

Areas of challenge: David has a difficult time with social situations. Things like changes in the schedule, moving from one activity to the next, or handling frustration can be very difficult for him. David also has a difficult time paying attention.

Diagnosis: David is diagnosed as having autism.

> Parents are an important part of the team at church. They are the most qualified experts the child has in your congregation. No information about a child should be given to others without the *written* permission of the child's parents or guardians. We've included a Sample Parent Permission Form on page 112.

David's Story

David was a very healthy baby who developed typically except in the area of speech. David's speech was quite delayed, and yet at 18 months, he knew all of the upper- and lower-case letters. He loved to watch videos. His parents had him evaluated by a team of developmental professionals, and they concluded that David might have Autism or something similar.

Children with Autism Spectrum Disorders (ASD) typically have differences in five areas. They often have more limited language ability and social skills, and they may get hooked on repetitive behaviors or themes. Their ability to interpret situations, feelings of others, and interactions may be limited. They may respond differently to sensations such as sound, light, and touch.

David attends Christian school, and his parents are excited to have found a church where David and his siblings will be educated and nurtured in the Lord. David has an older brother and sister as well as a younger sister.

Things you can do to support David: David needs a warm and welcoming place where he can enjoy being with his peers, understand more about who God is, and learn about Jesus' love for him.

Others who can help: Team members include David's parents, Tom and Nancy Bates, and Jody, coordinator of ministry to children and adults with special needs.

No information about an adult should be given to others without the *written* permission of the individual. If an adult is unable to give permission, you must obtain permission from the parent or guardian. We've included a Sample Adult Permission Form on page 113.

Specific Information About Adults with ASD for Adult Ministry Leaders

The coordinator for ministry to children and adults with special needs should contact the adult with ASD for more information. Using the interview questionnaire (see p. 109) as a basis, prepare a profile of the adult (see tips in sidebar on p. 45). Share a copy with the individual, and encourage him or her to reword the profile if desired or to add a personal note.

The sample profile on pages 53-54 is written for a thirty-six-year-old adult with Asperger Syndrome. The final section of this book includes a form you can attach to this profile to suggest specific strategies for leaders, including adult Sunday school teachers, Friendship leaders and mentors, and others who interact with this adult.

Presenting Angie

Profile written by Jody Kobes, coordinator of ministry to children and adults with special needs

Date: September 5, 2005

This profile is confidential information. Angie has given permission to share this with you to help you create a place for her to grow in Christ.

Programs Angie will attend this year: worship, adult Sunday school, Tuesday morning Women's Bible Study, and adult choir.

Interests, hobbies, gifts, and strengths: Angie enjoys going out for coffee with one other individual. She also really likes learning about computers. She is very good at understanding how they work and puts that to good use in her job in the medical records department at River Valley Hospital. Angie also enjoys music, especially music from the 1960s. Angie has a great vocabulary and an excellent memory.

Areas of challenge: Angie dislikes large crowds of people. The noise can be very frustrating to her. Angie is upset when people take coffee into the sanctuary even though a sign asks them not to do so. It's hard for her to even think about God when that happens. Angie also has a difficult time talking to more than one person at a time.

Diagnosis: Angie has been diagnosed with Asperger Syndrome.

Angie's Story

Angie grew up in a family with two brothers. She knew when she started junior high that something about her was different than the other children. Her parents noticed it much earlier, but no one was able to help them understand her needs. Angie did well in school academically, but she did not have many friends.

After high school, Angie took a job that involves using a computer to process medical records. She enjoys her job because she can work with just one supervisor.

One day Angie read an article in the paper about Asperger Syndrome. That gave her a word to describe her gifts and her needs. A psychologist agreed with Angie's self-diagnosis. Angie wants people in our church to know that she has Asperger Syndrome so that she can develop closer friendships.

People with Asperger Syndrome have an Autism Spectrum Disorder (ASD). They typically have differences in two or three areas. Although an individual with ASD will have a good IQ and vocabulary, they do not always understand social situations and may get hooked on repetitive behaviors or themes. They may respond differently to sensations— sounds can be too loud or soft, light can be too bright or dark, touch can feel different.

Things Angie desires in her faith community: Angie wants to go out for coffee one at a time with people from church. She wants to help other people when their computers break down. She wants people to know about Asperger Syndrome, and she wants people to stop breaking the coffee rule!

Others who can help: Team members include Angie and Jody, coordinator of ministry to children and adults with special needs.

Information for Peers of Children with ASD in Children's Ministry

The best way to help children include children with disabilities is to teach them about the disability. Following are some general guidelines for presenting information to peers:

- Present information about a child with special needs *with the child present*. This teaches children that the impairment is something they can discuss openly.
- Be positive and honest.
- Seek input from a parent or guardian before choosing what to share with the class.
- Get written permission from the child's parents [or guardian] before sending a letter home to the families of the child's classmates. . . . Personalize the letter to reflect the child's special needs.
- Keep communicating. One burst of information is not enough. You will need to talk openly throughout the year.
- Set aside special times to talk about God's attitude toward those with impairments.
- Use good children's literature to launch discussion.
- Send notes home occasionally to encourage the child and the child's parents.
- Be specific in your feedback with children [the child's peers] about an interaction.
- Encourage friendship.

—Barbara Newman, *Helping Kids Include Kids with Disabilities.* © 2001, Faith Alive Christian Resources, 2850 Kalamazoo Ave. SE, Grand Rapids, MI 49560. All rights reserved.

Along with presenting a lesson about ASD, you may want to read a book about ASD to the children. Check your local library or agencies in your community who work with children with ASD. After you've read the book, personalize the story by inserting the name of the child with ASD. With parental permission, talk about this child's gifts and needs. Talk about how friends can be excited about this child's gifts, and about specific ways they can help their friend with ASD.

For older children and youth, you might use a movie clip to show some of the differences in persons with ASD. Although I do not recommend watching the entire movie because of the language and sexual themes, one clip from the movie *Rain Man* is excellent. When his brother and girlfriend are visiting Dustin Hoffman in his room, you will be able to note the differences in language, social skills, repetitive themes and behaviors, and sensory responses. Use that clip to launch a discussion about including the child or youth with ASD. It's important to mention that ASD comes in a spectrum. Not all people look the same, but you can compare gifts and needs and highlight how friends can support one another.

The book *Helping Kids Include Kids with Disabilities* includes a complete lesson plan you can use to teach a child's peers about ASD. Also included is a letter that can be adapted for parents of peers.

Information for Peers of Adults with ASD

If the individual gives permission or you have the permission of the adult's guardian, you may want to more broadly distribute the profile you prepared. Adapt the profile so that it's not addressed just to leaders.

Suggest making the topic of celebrating diversity within the body of Christ a matter for a Sunday worship service. Center the service on passages like 1 Corinthians 12 or Psalm 139. (See sections 1-3 for some ideas.) Consider inviting an expert in the field of ASD to speak as part of this service. If done positively and honestly, it might be appropriate to introduce an individual with special needs who is part of your congregation. Remember, to best honor this individual, always start with the person's gifts and strengths.

Many churches offer Sunday school or adult education classes. You may wish to highlight the topic of special needs in a small group format. Ask individuals to share how they have been blessed by interacting with persons who have special needs. You may wish to invite a person who has ASD to share personal experiences and answer questions.

To teach peers about Asperger Disorder, you may wish to use the instructional DVD *Diagnosis Asperger's: Nick Dubin's Journey of Self-Discovery*. To request a copy, contact The Gray Center for Social Learning and Understanding, 4123 Embassy Dr. SE, Kentwood, MI 49546 (616-954-9747). You'll want to preview the DVD to be sure it's appropriate for the age level you wish to reach.

Elements of a worship service can cause distress for children and adults with ASD. They may express their distress by making noises during a quiet time, by leaving abruptly, or in some other disruptive way. Although it's important for leaders to figure out how to support the person with ASD, the entire congregation might benefit from information as well. My favorite example of this happened in a church my family was visiting.

My Friend Marie

It was time in the worship service for the pastor to give the message. As the pastor began to speak, an individual started making noise in the back of the church. Without missing a beat, the pastor calmly said, "Some of you might be hearing my friend Marie. Marie's mom and dad have asked me to tell you that she has autism. Sometimes the tags in her clothes or a sound she hears really bother her. I appreciate that Marie is my cheering section today."

The pastor continued with his message, Marie calmed down, and the congregation gave a collective sigh of relief. When Marie started a second round of "cheering" a little later on, no one seemed to notice the distraction.

It was important that Marie's pastor knew what to say and do, but it was equally important for Marie's faith family to know what was happening. Note that the pastor had communicated earlier with Marie's parents and had permission to share specific information, but he could have said something more broad:

Each one of us is wired differently. Many of us easily participate in worship each week. Others find it challenging to respond to all the people and sounds. So if someone needs to move around or call out at a time when others are quiet, let's remember that God gave the body of Christ lots of diversity.

The Ongoing Need for Information

Once is not enough. It's important to start off with good information, but you'll need to update people along the way. Children need chances to celebrate growth in a friend, and they also need to have the chance to talk about concerns. Adults need a chance to process information and an opportunity to ask questions or raise joys or concerns. The coordinator for ministry to children and adults with special needs can be invaluable in reading the tone of the church and keeping people informed as needed. If you have a larger number of individuals with ASD, consider forming a committee to support the coordinator and to handle specific needs for information.

Strategy 3: **Monitoring Sensory Input in Your Church Environment**

As we've discussed, gathering and sharing information are two key strategies that apply in every situation. Of the eight remaining strategies, this third strategy is likely to provide the most relief and the answers to many issues that come up each day with a person who has ASD. Understanding how individuals with ASD respond to sensory input enables us to adjust that input to their needs and limitations. Before looking at the techniques described here, you may want to go back to section 3 (pp. 36-37) and read about differences in sensory response in children and adults with ASD.

Healing Touch

The parents of a four-year-old boy with autism answered the call of a visiting evangelist: "If you desire prayer for healing, please come forward." Knowing that God can heal, they went forward, hoping for God's healing touch for their nonverbal son.

The little boy went willingly with his mom and dad to meet the prayer teams at the front of the church. Then the music got a bit louder. Those praying for the boy put their hands on him and started speaking loudly to overcome the volume of the worship band. The boy started to scream. As the prayers got louder and the crowd at the front got larger, the boy became more and more upset.

The parents finally left with the child. They felt for weeks afterward that others judged them to be sinful parents. After all, the boy wasn't healed that night.

Why did the child scream as people prayed for him? The child's actions are best explained by differences in sensory response. He was being touched by too many people. Touch registers very differently for this young boy. He also equates loud noise as a painful experience. When the music and voices kept getting louder, the pain intensified, and the boy communicated in a very efficient way by screaming.

A Basic Understanding

Our bodies are bombarded with sensory input all the time. In general, our receptors for sensory input are set at middle C on a piano or keyboard. Being in the middle is a great place to be. It allows us to block out a lot of unimportant sounds, sights, tastes, smells, muscle feedback, gravity feedback, and touch. Being at middle C lets unimportant things pass us by so that we are free to concentrate on what needs our attention. On the other hand, it also allows us to tune in to sensory input when needed. Although the dog snoring might not put us on alert, the sound of the baby crying might. Although someone brushing past us in the supermarket may not register, the hot teakettle in our hand will. Middle C is a great place to be most of the time.

Some individuals' sensory response system is set way above middle C. The slightest noise, touch, or sound registers immediately. These individuals might cover their ears to escape the pain of a sound. They might find a gentle hug unpleasant. The feel of a tag in the neck of a shirt may be intolerable. Children with an above middle C response often stand alone at recess. Adults may avoid coffee fellowship because of the commotion and sounds. Although therapists have come up with ideas to help soothe and try to bring these individuals down an octave or two, busy and noisy places are often unpleasant for them.

On the other hand, some people have sensory response systems that are set way below middle C. It takes a lot of sensory input for these people to register a response. Only louder noises rouse them. They may not notice pain even when they realize that a car door has shut on their hand. These people crave intense sensory input. Children may roll around, bang into people, use very loud voices, and use exaggerated and large movements. Children and adults often invade the territory of others around them in an effort to satisfy the sensory needs they have. Once again, professionals have found ways to try to get people in this category closer to middle C.

As you can see, we all have a fluctuating meter for receiving sensory input. If you have a headache, your set point automatically goes above middle C; everything is too loud and too bright. If you go to an exciting baseball game, your set point ventures below middle C where screaming and large movements become the norm. You find yourself participating in ways that would typically not happen. For some people with ASD, the set point is more rigid. The following strategies can be effective for these individuals, particularly those above middle C.

To learn more about differences in sensory responses, read *The Out-of-Sync Child* by Carol Kranowitz (© 1998, The Berkley Publishing Group). Even though this book discusses a wider range of individuals than those with ASD, the information is certainly helpful in understanding someone on the spectrum.

Provide a "Reset" Area

It is helpful to compare our sensory system to a computer. Even the best computers sometimes crash. When that happens, pushing the reset button clears off the old information and allows the computer to function again. Some people really need a place to reset their sensory system. Perhaps your church has a prayer room, a cry room, or similar small area with limited sound, sparse decoration, and few other people. (Even a bathroom can provide a quiet haven.) Let an individual with ASD know that this room is available anytime he or she needs a break—perhaps during coffee time or when the worship music gets too loud.

Consider providing this space with a rocking chair, as some people find the rocking motion calming. Some may appreciate having a cupboard or box where they could store objects they find calming: a special bottle of lotion, a CD player with a particular CD, a hairbrush. Check with the individual or with parents or caregivers to see if any other type of furniture or items could be helpful.

Try Break Time Instead of Time Out

For some children, the discipline tool we call "time out" may be scary or inappropriate. Imagine having a poor concept of the passage of time and then being pulled out of your routine to sit somewhere unfamiliar. (We'll talk more about this when we discuss strategy 6: Using Advance Warning Systems, pp. 75-80.)

Here's a similar idea for children who may need a place to push that "reset" button: Instead of using the phrase *time out,* consider using the words *break time.* If a child becomes anxious, moves around a lot, starts talking at a higher pitch, or demonstrates other signs of anxiety, you might ask if the child needs a break. Set apart an area where the sensations can be subdued. If you choose an area outside the room, make sure the child is comfortable in that place and that supervision is available. Let the child know that when he feels more comfortable, he is welcome to return at any time.

In contrast to a time out, break times are not a punishment. They are a tool to allow the individual to gain composure over the sensory system that is nowhere near middle C. Obviously adults are past the time-out stage, but adults with ASD can benefit from break time, which is a dignified way to regain composure.

Break Ticket

A child I'll call Noah did very well with all the class activities, but at times he needed a break from the regular classroom. Aside from social coaching, this is all the intervention we offered this bright child with autism. Noah had a "break ticket" in his classroom. He either chose to pick up the ticket himself, or the teacher would hand him the ticket when it was obvious he needed a break.

Noah knew that this break ticket meant he could come into my room to an area we had designated for breaks. Whenever he came in, I asked, "Noah, how long will your break be?" Noah would answer me with a time. When that time rolled around, he simply got up and went back to his classroom.

Forget Eye Contact

I have done it myself. A child misbehaves or gets upset, and the first thing I say is "look at me." This may not be a good plan for a person with ASD. Although some have mastered eye contact and can use it effectively when calm, it is a mistake to insist on eye contact when a person is coping with sensory overload.

One way to lessen the stimulation that is bombarding a person is to block some of it out. By averting the eyes, the visual input is removed, and the person can concentrate on the auditory input. When a person with sensory concerns gets upset, it's probably not the time to talk to, look at, or lightly touch the individual. Instead it's better to wait until the child or adult is calm.

Weigh the Effects of Touch

What is soothing for one person may not be soothing to another. Many—although not all—people with ASD react negatively to light touch. Instead of a feathery, light backrub, a person may more enjoy a hard and solid touch on the shoulders. It appears that the place in the

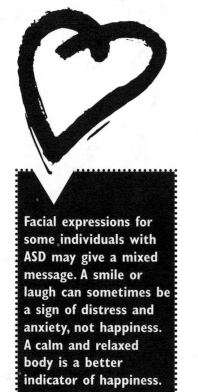

brain that registers light touch and pain are closely related. If a person's sensory system is not properly aligned, light touch registers as pain. Heavy or steady touch registers more positively.

Based on my experiences, providing hard or "rough" touch when a person is getting upset or anxious can be a very positive treatment. Although you will want to know the individual well, sometimes pushing down on a person's shoulders can be helpful. It lets that individual know her body is grounded. Another person might like a hard lotion rub on his arms. This can give calming feedback for some people. Many occupational therapists use a technique with a special brush. If this is effective for an individual, it might help to be trained in this technique, but only use it if indicated by a caregiver. The treatment appears to last about two hours. If your youth group, for example, is having a longer event, you might want to include this as part of your routine.

Try Headphones and Sound Blockers

Used in the worship center or a classroom, headphones and sound blockers can be helpful for many children and adults who are sensitive to loud or sudden sounds. Sometimes even having them available allows an individual to be calmer. Sounds that might not be loud to you may be painful to a person with auditory sensitivity. Imagine attending church with a migraine—that may help you be more understanding.

Headphones can play soothing music, or they can function as sound blockers and simply dull the noise. My classroom has several pairs of larger headphones with the cords clipped that work well to filter sounds. Some companies make headphones for people in the construction business; others are producing sophisticated headphones that block out background noise and accentuate the speaker's voice, a device that can be very helpful in a worship service.

Church education teachers may need to insist on a quieter environment. While giving the group more information about a friend with an auditory sensitivity, stress that one way to help is by using quieter voices. Not only may this be helpful for the individual, it might be an advantage for the whole group.

For adults with auditory needs or individuals with hearing aids, larger and louder places can be very confusing. A church might consider designating two coffee areas: one a larger mingling area, the other a smaller quiet room with a few tables and chairs. This would provide an option for persons who need a calm place to enjoy quiet conversation.

Add Rocking Chairs and Trampolines

The first year I served a student with autism, my classroom furnishings completely changed from very traditional furniture to a variety of items not typically found in a classroom. Although you'll want to research what an individual may prefer, a rocking chair and a mini-trampoline top my list of items you might find helpful.

Both seem to serve as medicine to an overloaded sensory system. For an individual unable to sit through a worship service, try replacing a chair with a rocker to allow a person to better focus on the service. (Make sure it's not a squeaky rocker.) To satisfy fire codes, you may need to place it in the pew cut out for people who use wheelchairs.

A rocking chair set in a break area or corner of a Sunday school classroom or Friendship meeting room can be helpful too. A child or adult who was previously unable to endure the louder group worship time may be able to enjoy it from a rocking chair placed slightly to the back of the room. The movement seems to override the louder noises and allows the individual to still be part of the group.

For children or adults who seem to be getting anxious or who need to move, a mini-trampoline can be a very helpful break activity. If a person has a difficult time sitting through a church service or group activity, place a mini-trampoline in the corner of a little-used room. The individual who needs a break can go there for a few minutes of hard and fast sensory input. This often allows an individual to quickly get back on schedule.

Plan for In, On, Under, and Through

Many Sunday school teachers have reported that a child with ASD will suddenly dive under a table or crawl into a small space. Unsure what to do, the teacher might label this action as misbehavior and react accordingly.

Although each person is wired differently, some enjoy being tucked away in a small place. Some individuals enjoy sitting on a bean bag chair and having one placed on top of them as well. Some people enjoy being rolled up in a carpet or having a refrigerator box to use as a safe haven. It's best to gather this information in advance and come up with a plan to make sure the person with ASD and the child's peers know about this need. Most individuals will sense when they can return to the scheduled events.

Some schools and other organizations have areas called sensory rooms. These places often contain swings, trampolines, ball pits, and other items used to provide sensory relief to overloaded systems. Most of these areas are organized and supervised by an occupational therapist (OT). A church that wants to provide a similar type of room should seek the direction of a professional. Expertise, safety, supervision, and insurance protection are important issues to consider.

The common items I have listed here can be used without the expertise of an OT and may or may not be successful for an individual.

Many persons with ASD have found relief by limiting certain food groups, such as breads. Several books highlight diets that are gluten-free. If an individual is not allowed to have gluten, then the traditional bread served at communion may not be an option and you'll need to make or buy gluten-free bread. Investigate solutions so that you can offer communion as an inclusive experience for everyone. You'll also want to consider other special dietary needs when planning coffee fellowship time, church potlucks, and so on.

Be Aware

The most helpful advice I can give for meeting the sensory needs of children and adults with ASD is this: think along with an individual. When you announce an all-church potluck, why is the individual with ASD getting upset? Try to gather information. What can you do to set up that activity to be successful for each person? Is it time for the Sunday school play? How can that child participate successfully? Is a Friendship group attending a play or performance? How can that individual feel comfortable in a new setting? Think in terms of sights, sounds, smells, and other sensory input.

Strategy 4: **Thinking Alongside the Person with ASD**

When children and adults with ASD are part of your faith community, you may observe situations like these:

- An adult on the way to Friendship class stops in the hallway and freezes. She refuses to move forward.
- A typically calm man begins to get very agitated in the worship service and starts calling out, "Stop!"
- A woman is unwilling to enter a particular room in the building and seems almost frightened of that particular place.
- A boy in Sunday school starts screaming and covering his ears nearly every time the group comes together for worship.

Leaders often contact me for ideas or suggestions to meet the special needs identified in situations like these. The strategy I generally suggest is to think alongside the individual with ASD. We'll look at how to help children and adults who are unable to express what is wrong and at ways to help those who can communicate their concerns and also introduce the idea of mentoring.

Thinking Alongside the Person Unable to Express Concerns

Some individuals with ASD may not have the ability to speak. Others may have good speech, but they are unable to answer the question What is bothering you? or What's wrong?

As you may recall from section 3, perspective-taking ability can be difficult for a person with Autism Spectrum Disorders, but it is likely one of your strengths. To use this skill, hop inside the head of the person with ASD. You will need to combine this third strategy with strategy 1: gathering information about the person with ASD. You may want to jot down your ideas as you think through these questions:

- What happened immediately preceding the incident?
- What happened right after the incident?
- What might the child or adult have seen?
- What might the person have heard?
- What might the person have touched?
- What might the individual have smelled or tasted?
- Who else is part of the setting?
- Has this happened before, or is it a one-time incident?
- Who else might be able to share insights into this person's behavior?
- What other things did you observe during this incident?

Once you have thought through this list, you will be better able to try some techniques that could help. The following situations provide some examples.

Frozen in Place

A woman we'll call Amanda always stopped at a crossroads in the church hallway. If she turned left, she would be led to the room where her Friendship group met. If she turned right, she would be directed to the worship center.

Since Amanda is unable to calculate days of the week, we suspected that she was confused about which way to go. Her solution was to stop and freeze. We asked her caregiver to present her with a Friendship take-home paper before entering the church. The caregiver told her to take the paper to Amy, her Friendship mentor. These basic prompts allowed Amanda to find the correct room without a problem.

This was our second attempt to find a solution for Amanda. Our first solution centered on inadequate lighting at that corner. Since placing a different light at that place in the hall did not help the situation, we had to try again. Many times it will take two or three guesses before you find the correct solution.

"Stop!"

Helping a man I'll call Damon required a group brainstorming session. Damon had never before called out Stop! during the worship service— his continuing outbursts were a complete surprise to everyone.

We thought through the list of questions. This never happened in winter, only in late spring and summer. It did not happen during worship time, only when the sanctuary was more quiet. We knew that Damon was sensitive to certain sounds, so we listened very carefully.

Meanwhile, we asked a friend to take Damon to the coffee break area when he became agitated. After a few weeks, we heard the problem—a lawnmower starting up across the street. A new person had moved into the neighborhood and had chosen to mow the lawn on Sunday mornings. After confirming that it was this noise that unsettled Damon, we asked his permission to speak to the neighbor. When the neighbor understood the issue, he was more than happy to wait until after the service to mow. Had he not been willing to accommodate Damon, we would have tried a noise-blocking device.

The Spooky Room

We tried several ideas to remove the fear of a particular room expressed by a woman I'll call Irene. We changed lighting, furniture, decorations, and leaders. Nothing worked! Finally we moved Irene's small group to a different room in the building. For reasons that remain a mystery, this was an immediate success!

Too Loud!

After thinking through the situation with a boy I'll call Zach, we realized that the volume in the room was simply too loud for him. More than a certain level of noise seemed to cause Zach pain.

As soon as Zach started screaming, a Sunday school teacher's helper would go with him to get a drink of water. Then they would return to the room together.

It seemed logical to offer Zach a chance to leave before he experienced pain. We made a card with a picture of a drinking fountain, and attached the card to a necklace Zach wore each week. Whenever the noise got too loud, he showed the card to one of the teachers and left the room to get a drink. He came back when the noise level was tolerable for him.

This has worked so well that Zach now leaves the room less frequently. Simply having the card provides security for him.

Don't be afraid of silence when speaking to a person with ASD. When you ask a verbal question or are expecting a verbal response, sometimes it takes extra time for the person to understand and form a response. It may help to ask a question and then slowly count to ten in your head.

These examples show that thinking along with an individual will often lead to solutions. Sometimes you can alter the environment, other times you can alter schedules or the actions of other people. Sometimes the individual can make changes that are helpful. By thinking along with someone, you can create many good choices and improve your own perspective-taking ability.

Thinking Alongside People Able to Express Concerns

Thinking alongside a child or adult who can express concerns verbally or in writing can still be a helpful skill. Many times individuals with ASD don't know which person to tell or are uncomfortable doing so. Sometimes another individual can help clarify the situation.

If you notice that a person is agitated, unusually quiet, or is showing some other type of discomfort, ask him or her if something is wrong.

In some cases, it helps to draw a face on a piece of paper showing a simple drawing of an irritated or upset expression. Show the face to the child or adult and say something like this: "You look upset. Can you tell me why?" Hand the person the drawing and a pen to write a response, or wait until the individual begins to talk. Sometimes the drawing cue can be a very helpful way to start a conversation.

Using a Mentor System

Sometimes it's helpful to have a group of four or five people who serve as mentors assigned to think alongside individuals with ASD, whether these are adults in a worship service or children in a Sunday school class. These people will get to know the individual and then take turns serving as a mentor. Many times parents play that role with children in a worship service, but the need for a mentor may also extend to other settings.

Mentors can serve in many ways. For example, an adult with ASD may be fearful of shaking hands with others. At that point in the service, the mentor might stay seated with the individual or discourage others from shaking hands. Perhaps the mentor could carry disinfectant wipes for the friend to use if this provides relief before and after shaking hands. If a squeaky microphone is a big problem for a person with ASD, the mentor may suggest leaving the service for a cup of coffee or a drink of water. If the pastor uses a phrase or illustration that is confusing to a child with ASD, the mentor can draw a picture or write notes to clarify the message.

> Show caution when assigning siblings as mentors to a child with ASD. Many siblings do a great job, but they are asked to fill that role so often. Perhaps your church can be a place where others can fill that role, and siblings can enjoy other friends for a time. Because being a sibling of a person with ASD carries some unique stresses, it's important for leaders of the siblings to be understanding. Siblings need trusted leaders who can allow them to be honest about their feelings and family situation.

Staying Put

A teenager I'll call Jordan has autism. Jordan likes to sit in the same area during worship and feels comfortable if the routine is familiar.

One Sunday the pastor talked about "going outside of our comfort zones for Jesus." To illustrate, he asked worshipers to stand up and relocate to a different part of the sanctuary. Jordan's mentor knew immediately that this would cause undue stress. Seated together, they stayed right where they were while others moved around them. Not aware of Jordan's special needs, some people made negative comments, but Jordan's mentor simply explained that this activity wasn't helpful for his friend.

In a Sunday school class, a child may not need a mentor all of the time, but one of the people in the room might be assigned to think alongside that child. It might even be a peer who knows that individual well. Children in first grade on up can do an awesome job if they're given critical information.

Some individuals with ASD who are aware that they don't always make great social decisions might appreciate having a team of mentors who can give them feedback. Teens or adults will especially benefit from having a mentor who can help them process situations that might occur at school, work, church, or in their neighborhood. The mentor team could give honest feedback and serve much like an accountability group. For example, a person might call or e-mail one of the mentors and describe a problem with a boss. The mentor tries to figure out what happened, how the boss perceived the situation, and how the individual with ASD perceived the situation. By sharing the perspective of the boss, it might help the individual with ASD know how to approach work the next day. Remember that some people with ASD have limited perspective-taking ability and may be unable to get inside the employer's head.

At times it might be uncomfortable to give such honest feedback to a friend with ASD. Keep in mind that words that might hurt your feelings could really be helpful information for another individual. For example, a mentor might notice a cue that a conversation with another person should end. The mentor might say, "Angie is looking around. I think she's telling you that it's time to get her child from nursery. She needs to stop talking now." Most people with ASD would find that helpful information.

All of us appreciate feedback that is given in a loving way. People with ASD need us to make an even more conscious effort to think alongside them and give them feedback that will help them function more comfortably in our faith community.

Strategy 5: **Making Routines Comfortable**

Imagine traveling to a foreign country where you do not know the environment or speak the language. You'll need a tour guide to find the best coffee shop and the most interesting sites to visit, decipher the train schedule, purchase food and supplies, and so on. Once you've memorized these important details, you'll be comfortable in your new environment. But what if the details change? What if the train schedule changes mid-day? What if the grocery store suddenly closes? Until you can piece together a new routine, you may feel a sense of panic.

That's how many children and adults with Autism Spectrum Disorders feel when familiar routines change. Because their senses, especially hearing, may not be able to process everything that is happening around them, they rely on routines to give structure to the day.

This fifth strategy will help you provide a secure environment for children and adults with ASD by creating comfortable routines.

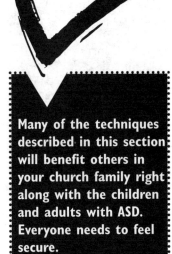

Many of the techniques described in this section will benefit others in your church family right along with the children and adults with ASD. Everyone needs to feel secure.

Printed Order of Worship

Many churches print some type of order of worship that describes the sequence of events in a worship service. These details can be very helpful for an individual with ASD.

I visited a church that used PowerPoint to list the order of worship from top to bottom on a large screen. The entire list was available at all times; the current item was highlighted in red as the congregation proceeded through the list. This is a great tool for a person with ASD.

Many churches provide a very detailed list of what will happen and at what time for people in the sound booth, the worship team, and the pastors to use during worship. It might be helpful to make an extra copy of this list for individuals with ASD.

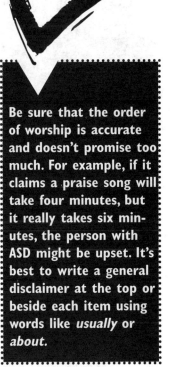

Be sure that the order of worship is accurate and doesn't promise too much. For example, if it claims a praise song will take four minutes, but it really takes six minutes, the person with ASD might be upset. It's best to write a general disclaimer at the top or beside each item using words like *usually* or *about*.

Picture Schedules

Many classroom teachers use picture schedules. For example, a set of pictures may show preschool children a sequence of activities as illustrated below. By placing pictures on separate cards, teachers can turn over one picture as an activity is completed. (We'll talk more about this when we describe how to use advance warning systems (strategy 6, pp. 75-80.)

This tool could easily be used with a nonreader in a worship service. To illustrate the order of worship, you might have a picture of a piano, praying hands, a singing face, a Bible, a stick figure speaking, an offering plate, stick figures greeting each other, and so on. These illustrations could be displayed on PowerPoint for all to see, or they could be drawn on numbered cards for an individual to use alone or with the help of a parent or mentor.

Picture schedules can be helpful in any setting where established routines and rituals are followed. Use a word or picture to represent the activities included in Sunday school, Friendship group, youth group meetings, small group Bible studies, and so on. Seeing the schedule gives a person with ASD the security of knowing what to expect.

It won't be necessary to make a new picture schedule each time something in the routine changes. Velcro saves the day for me! Just follow these steps:

- Laminate pictures for the activities that are generally a part of your routine. Cut them apart and put a strip of Velcro (the barbed side) on the back of each one. (This allows the picture to stick to flannelgraph boards, some fabrics, and even carpet squares.)
- Keep a few blank cards so that you can draw pictures or write a word or two to describe new activities that will be part of a particular day's schedule.
- Have the pictures available so that you can simply arrange them each week.

If you prefer not to use Velcro, teacher supply stores sell hanging pocket charts that allow you to arrange pictures in individual pockets. Or you could make pictures the size of baseball cards and insert them in plastic trading card sheets available in most toy departments.

Transition Techniques

Entering a room that is unfamiliar or filled with people can be very upsetting to people with ASD. It's good to have the same person greet a child or adult with ASD each time they come. Many times it helps to have the person be the first one inside and then assimilate others as they arrive. If that's not possible, it may also help to have a reserved seat for an adult or a special carpet square for a child to find as soon as they enter the room. If the person is comfortable with a particular chair or carpet square, you can move that item from one room to the next to make the transition easier.

As a person transitions from one area or activity to another, it might also be helpful to routinely give the person something to carry to the new environment. By giving a child a box of crayons to take to the craft table or room, the focus shifts from moving one's body to simply moving the box of crayons. To ease an adult's transfer from the worship center to the fellowship room, try handing the person an empty cup. Or give a person in a Friendship group a take-home paper to signal that it's time for the one-on-one session. This lets the individual know what's next and enables him to focus on moving the cup or paper rather than on moving his body.

The need to ease transitions may decrease as the person with ASD becomes comfortable in the environment. Remember, though, that if the schedule is changed or the environment is remodeled, you may need to use them again for a time.

Service as Part of the Routine

Each one of us needs to use the gifts God has given us. Although there should be many other opportunities for service, it's helpful to weave acts of service into the routine at church. For example, a person with ASD may enjoy coming to church early to prepare coffee for the fellowship time. Or she may enjoy coming to Tuesday morning Bible study one hour early to clean toys in the nursery, vacuum the foyer, restock library books, organize the bookstore, or collect bulletins from the pews. Including acts of service as part of a routine provides ongoing opportunities to serve.

In finding areas of service, take into account the abilities and interests of the individual. Although we may assume that a person on the spectrum would not enjoy being a greeter in church, we must remember that each person is unique. I know a young man with autism who greets every Sunday, shaking hands and passing out bulletins.

Once you have found a position that the individual will enjoy, you may need to offer some training. If the person with ASD will be organizing the books in the bookstore or helping to take money from people, good instructions should be given, preferably in writing or with pictures. Pair the person with a mentor or another worker and have them work together until you are confident the position will be a success for all involved.

For a variety of reasons, life for an individual with ASD can be difficult at times. Making routines comfortable and predictable goes a long way toward restoring peace and security.

Strategy 6: Using Advance Warning Systems

Retail stores understand this strategy well. The mall is about to close, employees are ready to go home, but shoppers are still lingering. A timely advance warning might remind them that the store is closing soon: "Shoppers, please make your selections. The store will be closing in ten minutes." A second warning establishes more boundaries: "Shoppers, please make your way to the check-out area. The store will be closing in five minutes." And finally, this: "The store is now closed. We hope you will return tomorrow."

This type of advance warning system is a strategy that's helpful to many persons with ASD. In this section, we'll look at two types of advance warning systems. The first is a way to measure time very concretely. The second is used when an existing routine will be changed.

Measuring Time Concretely

Persons with ASD often have difficulty measuring time. When I say, "I'll see you in a little while," many of my friends on the spectrum will not know what to expect. So it's important to give them a "heads up" about what is about to happen. In my church, for example, everyone knows that when the lights flash on and off in the fellowship area, it's time to go to the worship center; worship is about to begin. That's an advance warning system.

Be very careful when using a "time out" with persons with ASD. Although children may enjoy breaks from the action, placing a child who does not understand time in an isolated room can be very upsetting. For positive ways to give breaks, refer back to strategy 3: Monitoring Sensory Input in Our Church Environment (p. 60).

You Promised!

A friend at my church, whom I'll call Elizabeth, has autism. She really enjoys going out for coffee with friends. Because Elizabeth's autism affects her social skills and her ability to measure time, this was becoming an issue.

After only a brief conversation with others, Elizabeth often invited them to go out for coffee. She didn't know these people well, and they did not know her. Usually people would say, "Sure, let's go out some time." Or, "Let's do that soon."

Each time Elizabeth saw these people again, she reminded them of the promised coffee date. It was becoming uncomfortable for everyone, and Elizabeth was very disappointed that so many people broke their promises.

Instead of giving information to everyone else, I decided to structure time more concretely for Elizabeth. I suggested that before she could invite a friend out for coffee, she must talk with the person five times, each time on a different day. (Elizabeth has an amazing capacity to keep track of these things.) I also explained that when people say, "sometime" or "soon" that really means, "We will set up a time to go out and put it on our calendar." It might be this week or next month, but it will go on the calendar. This interpretation also allowed her to better understand the intent of the people she invites.

When my coffee date with Elizabeth is over, I drop her off and say, "We can go out for coffee again in July." Sure enough, on July 1, I will get a phone call from Elizabeth to put the date on our calendars.

You'll find ordering information for the Time Timer on page 133. The designer gave one to her pastor to help him watch the time as he's preaching. No church should be without at least one!

Use a Time Timer

When working with special needs students, I rely on a special clock called a Time Timer. A Time Timer does not make a loud ticking sound or give an auditory signal; instead this battery-operated tool gives a visual display of disappearing time. The timer is set by turning the dial; part of a red wheel appears to match the amount of time you indicate. As time disappears, so does the red part of the wheel. When the red is gone, time is up.

This visual reminder of passing time is helpful to indicate how long children will be in a large group worship setting before moving to their smaller Sunday school class. It can show a youth or adult in Friendship how long the group time will last before it's time for the one-on-one mentoring session. The timer can be used to signal a favorite activity. If a child loves snack time, you can set the timer. When the red is gone, it's time for a snack.

If you set the timer and then find everything is running ahead of schedule or a bit late, simply let the individual know that you need to reset the timer. You can then add or subtract time in a way that is generally easily understood by the person with ASD.

Give a Verbal Countdown
Another way you can structure time is by giving a verbal countdown for
events. For example, you might say, "In two minutes we will be going
to the worship center." Or, "In five minutes, it will be time to go home."
This helps put the transition in a context that is generally easy to
understand. Some individuals compute specific times like two minutes
without difficulty. Others might appreciate seeing the two minutes
disappear on the Time Timer. Either way, you've given them time to
prepare for the next activity.

Use a Picture or Word Schedule
As we discussed with strategy 5, a picture or word schedule can describe
a routine. It can also be used to mark passing time. Some individuals
appreciate removing the picture when the activity is done. Others might
turn the picture over or cross off the word when the activity is completed.
It's like having a "to do" list for that moment in time.

Use Concrete Language
We often use very obscure language when we discuss time concepts.
As we noted in Elizabeth's situation, words like *sometime, later, perhaps,*
and so on don't give much information.

"Talk to You Later!"

A young adult I'll call Caleb enjoys talking to my family on his cell
phone. Not always aware of the social rules about phone use, he called
several times an hour. After repeated calls, we realized that our words
were prompting his actions.

Every time we ended our conversation we said, "Talk to you later." For
me, these words mean *sometime,* but Caleb focused on our request and
called us later—two minutes later!

We finally thought of a better way to mark time. Now we say, "I'll talk to
you after supper" or "Call again tomorrow." When we mark time in a way
that is concrete, Caleb understands the parameters.

Use Brainstorming Sessions
As with other strategies, it's helpful to brainstorm with a group of people to find solutions. As you take what you know about the individual, you can then try some ideas that make sense in your setting.

Number 49

A boy I'll call Sam has autism. Sam became very upset each time the organist began to play.

Brainstorming together, a group of leaders in his church discovered that Sam really enjoys numbers. Their church uses a nursery call system where children are assigned a number. When a child's number flashes on the small screen, the child's parent is to come to the nursery. This innovative group decided to assign a number to Sam. Each time the organ is about to start, the number 49 flashes up on the screen. This gives Sam a few seconds to get ready for the sudden noise, and he no longer gets upset.

Signaling Change

Once a routine is in place, children and adults with ASD find that change can be very difficult. Some individuals react strongly even to the word *change*. You might see a person become very anxious or even aggressive when change is in the air. An advance warning system can structure an environment so that change is predictable and accepted.

Word Schedules Carefully
Imagine that you once had a difficult time structuring and understanding the passage of time. Then you learned how to tell time. When actual times are listed beside an activity, you can predict when things will happen. When those times are not honored, the one system you thought was predictable no longer makes any sense. That can cause confusion and consternation.

Use careful wording on your printed and picture schedules (see sidebar on p. 71) to avoid confusion. Some churches are very good about keeping to the listed time schedule; others have a more relaxed style. Many individuals with ASD can get upset about times that are not fulfilled. A simple wording change in the bulletin can be very helpful. For example, instead of saying an exact time, say: "Worship begins about 10:00 a.m." In classroom settings, you may have a printed or picture schedule on the wall with times. Either use approximate times *(about)* or remove the times and simply show a sequence of events. These simple changes can really allow some clock-watching individuals to calm down.

Make On-the-Spot Changes

If you are using a picture schedule, making last-minutes alterations to the day's schedule can be a very concrete act. If the individual has already seen the schedule, simply say something like this: "Oops, I need to move a few pictures around." When you make the change in front of the child or adult without using the word *change,* the person is more likely to accept the new schedule.

The same is true for word schedules. Without using the word *change,* you can write a new heading on the person's bulletin. Use a marker to write: *New and Improved Schedule for Sunday, May 10.* Then write in the new activities or new order of events. If you use PowerPoint, adapt it on the spot for the entire congregation.

Prepare for the Unexpected

If an activity will include something that is not usually part of the normal routine, it's helpful to give advance warning. For example, ending your Christmas Eve service with lighting individual candles is a change in routine that might upset some individuals with ASD. To warn them, you might place an announcement in the bulletin:

> **Next week our Christmas Eve service will begin at about 5:30. At the end of the service, after the benediction, each person will receive a candle. Choir members will light the candles, and then we will sing "Silent Night" with just the candles lit.**

If you prefer not to use a bulletin announcement, consider sending a card to the individual or use your church mailbox system. Or ask a mentor to add a word or picture card to the picture schedule of the worship service.

Sometimes changes come up suddenly, and you'll have no time to send out a card or prepare a bulletin announcement or picture. If this is the case, written or spoken words on the spot may be helpful. A pastor who has been speaking a bit long and will need to alter the ending schedule may say, "Since I needed a bit of extra time to finish my message, we will not sing the hymn. Instead, we will present our offering now."

This is another time where a mentor can ease the situation. Without using the word *change,* the mentor could quickly cross through the song on the printed bulletin or remove the song picture from the schedule. The PowerPoint operator would not highlight this section of the worship order.

Malls and five-star hotels find advance warning systems helpful for customers and guests. So why not use this strategy in our church environment too! Giving advance warning can add to the quality of interactions for children and adults with ASD.

Strategy 7: Closing the Communication Gap

As we discussed in section 3, individuals with ASD experience differences in language. Some individuals are nonverbal; others have difficulty with understanding directions or groups of words. Although it doesn't show up on typical language tests, some children and adults diagnosed with Asperger Syndrome have a hard time with the practical use of language. Conversations can be a challenge.

Many individuals struggle to understand language that is less concrete. For example, figures of speech and words with multiple meanings can be a huge challenge.

While writing this book, I came across an amazing book by Ian Stuart-Hamilton called *An Asperger Dictionary of Everyday Expressions* (Jessica Kingsley Publishers, 2004). This book has 240 pages of common phrases alphabetically arranged and translated into more literal language. For example, the book describes what people really mean when they say things like

- Join the club.
- That's a hard act to follow.
- I'll be a monkey's uncle.
- Pound the pavement.

Under the Weather

Recently I created a communication gap for a friend I'll call Jayden. As part of our conversation, Jayden asked a question about a phone call I had received while at his home. I told him that my sister was calling to tell me that my mom was a bit "under the weather." Jayden stared up at the sky, looked bewildered, and probably figured all of us were under the weather! His observant mother quickly interpreted: "We sometimes say people are *under the weather* when they are sick."

Like our social language, our faith language is also filled with an amazing number of analogies and figurative pictures. Even though we might not be able to close the communication gap entirely, strategy 6 will give you specific ways to make language more meaningful for people with ASD.

Plan Ahead

Often we can anticipate the need for translation. For example, the pastor's chosen Scripture passage and message title for the following week may be included in the bulletin. Sunday school teachers, adult education leaders, and Friendship mentors will know what the next lesson is about.

If the sermon or lesson is about the Beatitudes, for example, be ready to translate each one. When Jesus says, "Blessed are the poor in spirit, for theirs is the kingdom of heaven," Jesus is saying, "The person who is humble is happy, because the good things that are important to God belong to that person."

If you are teaching a Bible story, identify confusing phrases or words ahead of time. For example, the Old Testament talks a lot about *clean* and *unclean* animals. What does this mean? It doesn't mean that some animals have had a bath! Explain that God gave certain rules to his people about eating and worshiping; some animals were not to be eaten or used for sacrifice (an offering), and these animals were called *unclean.*

Often we use phrases like *covered with the blood of Jesus* or *give your heart to Jesus.* It's hard to give an invitation to accept Jesus without using any figurative language, but I've found this five-color technique helpful:

- The color gray reminds me that I do wrong things that make God sad. These wrong things are called *sins.* My sins keep me away from God.
- The color red reminds me that Jesus died on the cross for me. Jesus loved me so much that he was willing to shed his blood and die for me.
- The color white reminds me that Jesus took away my sins and made my heart clean and white as snow. Now I can be close to God again.
- The color green reminds me that Jesus is alive! And Jesus gives me new life so that I can be more like him every day.
- The color gold reminds me that Jesus is in heaven. If I love Jesus, I will live with him in heaven someday.

—The Easter Book: A Resource for Leaders and Mentors, © 2003, Faith Alive Christian Resources, Grand Rapids, MI 49506. All rights reserved.

Notice that we can still use words like *sin, blood, heart,* and *new life* as long as we explain them in more concrete ways.

The Easter Book was written by Barbara J. Newman as part of the Friendship Bible studies series, designed for youth and adults with cognitive impairments. The accompanying visuals for the five-color technique would be helpful for nonreaders, or you can simply use crayons or colored paper. This technique and others in the book can be adapted for those on the autism spectrum. The book is available from Friendship Ministries (1-888-866-8966) and at www.friendship.org.

Many times we cannot anticipate what words or phrases will confuse someone with ASD. We noted the value of mentors when describing strategy 4: Thinking Alongside the Person with ASD (see p. 69). While thinking along with that person, the mentor can translate confusing figures of speech by restating the phrase. For example, when the mentor or person with ASD hears a confusing phrase during worship or in an educational setting, the mentor can jot down or illustrate the meaning of that concept on a notepad. In conversation, a mentor could restate the part of the conversation that is confusing.

If the person with ASD has good reading and writing skills, the individual might write down parts of a sermon, lesson, or newsletter that were confusing, and then agree to meet later with a mentor or other designated person to discuss and clarify these items. This could lead to great fellowship and acceptance.

Check Your Written Materials

Read through the brochures and newsletters your church distributes. Consider whether someone with ASD will understand phrases like the following:

- faith community
- profession of faith
- holy communion
- Advent
- Lent
- sanctuary
- narthex

By translating phrases like these—and dozens more we use freely—you will support the needs of children and adults with ASD and at the same time make your church more welcoming to those unfamiliar with church jargon and religious terms.

Reach Those with Limited Verbal Skills

We could write an entire book of strategies for individuals who have limited verbal skills. I'll share just a few techniques.

Use Visuals
To enable a person who is nonverbal to participate in a praise and worship time, draw pictures for three or four favorite songs. Set those pictures in front of him and let him choose the song by handing you a picture. If you are telling a story about David and Goliath, have a picture in front of you for both characters. Ask questions about the story that can be answered by pointing to the picture of David or Goliath. Or use the pictures to cue the person with limited verbal skills to say the names as they appear in the story.

You'll find these versions of the Bible helpful when translating meanings for people with ASD:

- *New International Reader's Version* (International Bible Society), written at a third- or fourth-grade reading level.
- *New Century Version* (Word Publishing), written at a bit higher level.
- *New Living Translation* (Tyndale House Publishers, Inc.), written at the junior high reading level and intended to be understood by the average reader of modern English.

I've found that two different groups of people use sign language. The first group includes those who are hearing impaired and who use precise, grammatically structured hand movements to convey thoughts and ideas. American Sign Language is a language just like Spanish, German, and English are languages. The other group includes people who can hear but are limited verbally. They may use many of the same signs used by people who are hearing impaired but often use single signs or motions to represent a word or phrase. These signs are a tool for communicating; they are not a *language.*

Learn to Use Communication Devices

Some people with ASD use picture cards or a talking computer. It's important that the coordinator for ministry to children and adults with special needs, the Friendship mentor, Sunday school teacher, and other leaders become familiar with these devices. Parents and caregivers will appreciate your interest and be willing to help you adapt the system for worship, church education, and other settings in your church environment.

Learn and Use Signing

If some people with ASD use signs or hand gestures, it's important for church leaders to learn and use some of these signs. For example, if the individual knows the sign for *Jesus* or *Father,* the pastor can sign these words as they are said during worship. Children's ministry leaders and peers can sign along with the child with ASD. It's not necessary to sign every word to connect with an individual; simply sign some key words the individual knows.

By doing so you will communicate in a caring way with the individual who is nonverbal and probably draw in other members of your group at the same time. Many congregations are finding that signing can be a powerful and reverent opportunity for worshipers to participate.

Teach in Advance

It's important that individuals with limited language skills are given the opportunity to participate in group activities. For example, you can teach songs in advance that will be used routinely in your group worship time during the church education year or Friendship season. Share the printed music or recorded versions of the songs with parents or caregivers so that the child or adult with limited language can learn them over the summer. Even if the person can't sing all of the words, the individual will recognize a familiar tune and be able to sing along on a chorus or clap to the beat.

If memory work for several weeks is John 3:16, you might send a card home with just the first part: "For God so loved the world . . ." When the group recites the verse, your friend will have memorized the first part and can participate in this group activity. He or she might prompt the group to finish the rest of the verse.

Share How Individuals Communicate

Let others know how an individual communicates. Techniques we discussed under strategy 2 can be used to convey this information to leaders. Sometimes an informal conversation will be helpful.

Eyes That Talk

A woman in our church I'll call Maria has Cerebral Palsy. When Maria looks up and makes eye contact, she is saying yes. When she looks down or away, she is saying no. We asked her permission: "Can we tell people how you say yes and no with your eyes?" She looked right at us. Knowing this allows people to ask her questions and have a conversation with her during coffee time.

Enhance Understanding

Language isn't just about talking, it's also about understanding what we hear. Many times listening and understanding can be difficult for a person with ASD. Here are a few important tips to remember.

- Use shorter phrases. "David, come here" is easier to hear and understand than "I want to see David over here at my table area." If you combine the shorter phrase with a gesture or a picture of the place you want David to be, you'll have an even greater chance that David will understand your instructions.
- Avoid saying what you *don't* want a person to do. If an individual has limited language understanding and you say, "Don't touch the light," the person may have heard only the words *touch* and *light,* and end up doing exactly what you didn't want done. State only what you want the individual to do one step at a time: "Come here. Sit down. Fold your hands."
- Wait before repeating directions. The time it takes for an individual to process your question can be longer as well. If you say, "Becky, can you point to Goliath?" you might need to wait several seconds before her hand moves. It can be very confusing to a person if you just keep repeating the question: "Go ahead, point to Goliath. Do you see him right here? I'm pointing to Goliath, can you do it too?" You have most likely flooded an individual with so much language, that the system is overloaded. After you ask a question, be comfortable with silence. Once you have waited, you may then want to give an additional prompt.
- Visualize sequenced directions. Make a visual list if you have a sequence of directions for people to follow. Use sequenced pictures of crayons, scissors, and glue to tell a child to color the

Remember that people retain only about 30 percent of what they hear. People with ASD aren't the only ones who will benefit from sequenced directions!

picture, cut it out, and then glue it on the construction paper. When an adult worship leader, pastor, or Friendship leader gives directions for the opening activities, he or she might say, "Everyone please stand." When people are standing, the leader says, "Let's shake hands and greet people around us." Then the leader says, "Please take out the red songbooks and find page 54." That will be easier for most people to digest than "Let's stand, greet one another, and then sing the song found on page 54." A PowerPoint visual for each of these activities will give everyone a cue about the sequence of events.

Avoid Misunderstanding

Many times when an individual appears confused or even hurt, think through the language that was just used. The examples I have from my interaction with persons who have ASD could fill a huge book. Often, once the language is cleared up, everyone feels much better.

Carpet Squares

A preschool teacher greeted the class and said, "Everyone get a carpet square and sit down." Most children knew that meant that they should get a carpet square, come to the circle area, and sit down. But the teacher never said the middle part about coming to the circle. So the child with autism found a carpet square, sat down in the middle of the toy area, and started to play alone.

The teacher could have interpreted this child's action as misbehavior. Instead she repeated the directions, this time adding the circle part. The child quickly joined the other children at the circle area and felt like part of the group.

Before judging a person's motive, make sure your directions are clear. In my experience, most people with ASD want very much to follow instructions. Sometimes communication can be a huge roadblock.

Many people, especially teachers or other leaders, expect and insist on eye contact: "Eyes up here; look at me. I won't start until everyone is looking at me." Although most individuals with ASD are truly working on this area, many can concentrate more efficiently without making eye contact. The speaker's face often blocks out the spoken word, so the individual looks away to concentrate on language. Although educators know the importance of eye contact, we often teach individuals with ASD to look at the bridge of the nose or nose of another person. This allows an individual to concentrate on a stable facial feature so that one can digest the verbal information. Again, it's important to respect an individual's specific needs and situation. If a person listens to a Bible story better by looking at the floor, let the individual look at the floor. If a person with ASD is upset or screaming, that is not the time to insist on eye contact!

Whether written or spoken, words constantly bombard us. When listening and verbal skills are limited in some way, persons with ASD are easily left out of the learning and fellowship in our church life. To be a more welcoming church, it's important that we bridge the communication gap!

Strategy 8: Using Visuals to Reinforce What We Say

"If I didn't see it, you didn't say it!" Carol Gray, expert in the area of autism and founder of The Gray Center for Social Learning and Understanding in Kentwood, Michigan, used this phrase at one of her workshops. It is always in the front of my mind as I work with individuals with ASD. Most people on the spectrum require a visual of some sort to reinforce the spoken word.

The old saying that a picture is worth a thousand words might be our motto. Let's translate it literally: 1,000 words equals one picture. Use PowerPoint, videos, portraits, slides, overhead projectors, or real objects—at least one visual for every thousand words you speak.

Whether you are a Sunday school teacher, a Friendship mentor, a pastor, or a small group leader, use visuals. Most people in your congregation or group will enjoy them; children and adults with ASD need them.

Think in Pictures

If you are studying Ephesians 6 about putting on the armor of God, how could your message be summed up in a picture? Could an artist portray that for you? Could you put together a puzzle as you go through the passage?

Picture this passage from Isaiah 40:29-31:

> He gives strength to the weary, and increases the power of the weak. Even youths grow tired and weary, and young men stumble and fall; but those who hope in the Lord will renew their strength. They will soar on wings like eagles, they will run and not grow weary, they will walk and not be faint.

If you normally think in words, allow God to expand your mind's eye. Use the pictures God gives you to communicate with those who generally think in pictures. In fact, an individual with ASD may be able to provide some powerful pictures and images for you.

Use Paper and Pencil

Always have paper and a pencil available. This will allow you to sketch or write back and forth with an individual with ASD. For example, if a child is upset, I might avoid hugging or cuddling her but instead draw an upset face on a piece of paper. I'll hand her the drawing and say, "You look upset." Then the child can draw or write or speak a response to the visual cue.

Sometimes a person with good verbal skills has a problem you do not understand. In order to understand this person's perspective, I often say, "Tell me what happened." Instead of just listening, I begin to draw the situation on a piece of paper. Although I'm no artist, I use stick figures to set up the scene in a visual way. This often allows the person to fill in details of who is in the picture, where they were, and what happened. Many times the individual will take my pencil and add important details to the picture.

By writing down someone's thoughts or words, you are also indicating that you are listening and have heard what is said. For example, if a child asks repeatedly to take a game to church, you can simply get a sheet of paper and write, I want to bring my Game Boy to church. If the child is able, have the child sign his name to the sheet. Lay it on the table. If the child brings up the topic again, tap the paper and remind the child that you know. Once it is in writing, it will often bring a sense of calm to the child.

This can also be true in a small group discussion. Many times, a person with ASD will interrupt a discussion several times with questions or thoughts. Although it might be helpful to talk to the individual about this and suggest that two questions or comments per meeting is generally the rule for Bible studies, you might also like to record the individual's question or comment on a whiteboard or sheet of paper. This indicates you have heard the comments or questions. Even if you will be answering them later, acknowledging these comments on paper can often ease the person's mind.

Make Prayer Time Visual

Prayer time is generally verbal, so it's important to think about ways to make it visual and concrete for those who have difficulty with language.

If you are in a small group or a one-on-one setting, consider writing or drawing prayer requests on small notecards. Set an empty chair aside and mention that Jesus is a part of each prayer circle. Although Jesus doesn't need a chair, explain that the group will take these prayer requests to the chair when everyone is finished praying. That means Jesus has heard our prayer.

You can use prayer journals, prayer scrolls, or a prayer request board for recording requests and responses. Think of other ways to make prayer visual and concrete.

Some people may have the same prayer request over and over. If their request was only offered verbally, they may be unsure if God heard their request. They may need visual affirmation.

Alicia

A friend I'll call Alicia was struggling with forgiving another individual. Week after week, she came to several individuals requesting prayer about the person who had offended her. It finally dawned on me that we were only using verbal prayer with her.

One day God gave me insight to ask her to write the name of the person on the palm of my hand. As we prayed together for forgiveness, I asked her to move my hand away from her and toward God. As she did, I said, "Now that person and all of the things that happened belong to God. They don't belong to you anymore."

That visual prayer worked. In fact, it seemed to free her to pray powerfully for others. Many women in her Bible study go to her with their prayer requests, and God has given her helpful insights.

Don't Just Say It, Do It!

How can you make concepts like forgiveness, compassion, mercy, and justice, concrete and visual? Perhaps justice requires that you weigh something on a balance scale like those used in a science experiment. Forgiveness may require writing something down and then tearing it up or erasing it.

Let's think about the phrase *giving your heart to Jesus*. It's one of those phrases we use without thinking about the literal meaning people with ASD may give it. We gave a visual example of how to explain this phrase in strategy 7 (p. 82), but this time let's add actions. Place some paper hearts and a marker by a cross at the front of your church. Then say something like this:

> *(Hold up a paper heart, and place your hand over your heart.)* We often call a person's thoughts, feelings, words, and actions a person's heart. If you are sorry for the wrong things you do and believe that Jesus loves you, I invite you to give your heart to Jesus. Please come forward. *(Wait for people to come.)* Write your name on one of these paper hearts and tape it to the cross. *(Allow time for this action.)* By doing this, you are

telling God's family in this place that you love Jesus and want to serve him.

Use Visuals for Classroom Management

What benefits children with ASD in this area will help everyone, including the leader. We all know the teacher who repeatedly says, "It's time to be quiet." Usually the classroom is noisy a great deal of the time. A sign or picture that indicates it's time to be quiet will be much more effective. Some teachers use a traffic light cut-out and a clothespin. When the clothespin is on green, children can talk freely. When the clothespin is on yellow, children may talk in whispers. When the clothespin is on red, children must raise their hand to talk or talk silently to themselves. This visual gives a constant reminder of expectations.

As you arrange your room for a new season, take pictures of the books on shelves, toys in baskets, and so on. When you ask the children to clean up the room, show the pictures. Remind the children that the storage areas should look like the pictures when they are finished.

As we mentioned when discussing advance warning systems (see strategy 6, p. 76), the Time Timer is a visual way to mark the passage of time. No classroom with a child who has ASD should be without this tool. In fact, many younger children who do not yet understand time concepts will also appreciate this timer.

Another visual classroom management technique is to use a buddy system. Many children with ASD will quickly follow the lead of a good role model.

Don't Let Visuals Become Your Worst Enemy

Some children are so tuned in to the visual environment that your words may be overridden. If visuals say one thing, and your words or actions say another thing, the visuals will most likely rule the day. For example, if your PowerPoint schedule says that children can leave the service for their own worship time at 10:00, some children may leave promptly at 10:00 even if the service is running behind schedule.

Sometimes inaccurate pictures can be a problem. If you take a digital picture of children in praise and worship that doesn't include the child with ASD, that individual may not participate. Evaluate your environment. What's written or pictured may often become law. In order to counter that powerful input, you will need to visually override it.

Often an individual with ASD may have excellent visual skills and less acute auditory skills. In fact, this can be so pronounced that it will seem like one of those old movies where you see the picture, but the sound track isn't in sync with the speaker's mouth. When these two systems are out of line, watching and listening at the same time can be a unique problem.

My pastor frequently e-mails his sermon notes to a few people who will give ideas for illustrations, visuals, and other ways to connect with those wired in a more visual or experiential way. Seek out those in your church who are gifted in art, photography, graphic design, and so on to help you develop visuals that will benefit those with ASD and your entire church family.

Strategy 9: Writing Stories to Help People with ASD Anticipate New Situations

Although I don't claim to know much about sports teams, I am aware that a team often has a defensive role and an offensive role. The defense usually reacts to what is happening while the offense usually makes a plan and initiates the play. Most of the strategies in this book fall into one of those two categories. Defensive strategies, such as adjusting sensory input in our church environment and making routines comfortable, are used in reaction to the needs and behaviors of the person with ASD. Thinking alongside people with ASD and using advance warning systems are examples of offensive strategies. We set up the situation first so that an experience can be a good fit for the individual involved.

Writing stories is an example of an offensive strategy that can be a powerful tool for many people, not just those with ASD. If you can get one person in your congregation excited about this idea, you could have the most visitor- and member-friendly environment imaginable for both children and adults.

We'll use the term *stories* to describe a strategy that incorporates words and simple pictures or photos that depict an activity someone with ASD is about to participate in as part of your faith community. The story gives information in advance so that the situation is comfortable and welcoming.

Why Give Information in Advance?

As my mother was preparing for heart surgery, she received a booklet that told her exactly what would happen and what to expect before, during, and after surgery. Hospitals know that advance information can be calming for individuals.

Hospitals are not the only ones. Many larger retail stores produce store guides that tell exactly where items are located and how to find them. These guides let a person understand the layout of the place before setting foot in any aisle.

Whenever I speak at conferences and churches, I try to get as much advance information as possible. Not only is it helpful to have specifics about personal things, such as where I will sleep and eat, the times I will be working, and how I will travel from place to place, I also enjoy knowing in advance more about the organization and community. What's important to the church? What is the vision and mission of that organization? How can I enhance what God is doing in that community? Knowing these things in advance helps me prepare and relax concerning what is to come.

Most of us appreciate having some type of advance plan for new situations. Imagine how important the advance plan is for individuals who have a difficult time with social rules and conventions. Imagine entering a church where you can't automatically figure out how to act, what to wear, when to be quiet, what to do, or why an event may be taking

place. I suggest that churches write stories to help persons with ASD anticipate and be ready to interact in new situations. (For some illustrated examples, see pages 114-126 in the reproducible resources section of this book.)

Introducing a Child or an Adult to a New Class

Teachers of preschoolers will tell you that young children benefit from knowing what to expect about this brand-new experience. Stories can serve the same purpose for children and adults entering a new classroom experience at church.

Consider handing out a story describing the upcoming Sunday school class one to two weeks prior to the beginning of a new season. The story gives information about the format of the class and what to expect. It might include simple stick-figure pictures, or you may wish to take a photo of the room, layout, leaders, and other supplies and include it in the book. Remember to use photos of things the child will actually see. Every child enrolled in your program (and their families) will appreciate this information, and the child with ASD will benefit greatly.

A sample story introducing Sunday school to early elementary children is included on pages 114-115 in the reproducible resources section of this book. Adapt it to describe your particular program.

A sample story introducing an adult to a small group Bible study is included on pages 116-117 in the reproducible resources section of this book.

Perhaps you are starting a Friendship group or small group Bible study. Words and pictures can describe exactly what will happen and what someone attending might expect. Depending on the specific needs of the person with ASD, you may need to write a story just for the individual, or you may wish to write a story that will be helpful to everyone attending.

Explaining Changes in Programming

Likely every ongoing activity in your church will experience some type of change in schedule, format, staffing, and so on at some point during the year. As we've discussed earlier, children and adults with ASD often have difficulty handling change.

Instead of simply letting people show up and experience changes on the spot, stories can prepare them in advance. Use stories to describe field trips, service projects, parties, time off, summer programs, special services, and much more. Anything that interrupts the usual routine can be written in story form.

You'll find a sample story explaining the change in summer programming at my church on pages 118-120. Our summer church education program is quite different from our September to May program. I distribute this story to all the children who will be attending our summer adventure.

Describing Expected Behavior for Worship and Fellowship

Many churches have bulletins that routinely list the order of worship. In strategy 5, we discussed several techniques for giving additional information about the schedule to persons with ASD (see pp. 71-72). But some things aren't part of the schedule, and church leaders often mistakenly think everyone knows these things.

Many churches assume that people have attended a worship service before and that they can quickly adapt their behavior to fit in with the rest of the people in a specific setting. Persons with ASD—and many visitors too—find this assumption intimidating, and it keeps them from attending church and participating in the life of the church.

A story about the things that are not included in the bulletin can be distributed as a welcoming flier or brochure to everyone visiting, or it can be designed specifically for the person with ASD. For example, comments about dress, voice volume, singing, people saying "amen" during the service, greeting time, offering, baptism, communion, ministry, and more provide valuable information to those with ASD who can read.

As we noted earlier, our words, whether spoken or written, must say what we mean. For example, a pastor may announce that anyone needing prayer is welcome to see him after the service. In making this offer, a pastor is assuming that the same individual will not come forward after each and every service in response to that request. A person with ASD may not realize that this repeated response would monopolize the pastor and not allow others to participate.

Describing Specific Events

Faith communities celebrate significant religious events and develop rituals that build fellowship within the body. People with ASD benefit from stories that describe these events and rituals in advance. Members of your church could write stories to describe the church picnic, the Christmas Eve service, the joint outdoor worship service with another church, or communion and baptism.

You'll find a sample flier to describe expected behavior for worship and fellowship on pages 121-122 in the reproducible resources section of this book. Adapt this idea to meet the needs of the individual with ASD and to describe the expectations of your church community.

A sample story describing a communion service is included on page 123. You'll want to adapt this to the specific practices in your church. If your church celebrates communion every Sunday, the person with ASD may not need this story, but if the routine changes, be ready in advance to describe what will happen.

It's possible that you may want to write a story about becoming a Christian or expectations for membership in your church. In the booklet *Expressing Faith in Jesus: Church Membership for People with Cognitive Impairments,* author Ronald Vredeveld emphasizes the importance of walking alongside people as they prepare to become professing members of a church. Stories could be written to describe the preparation class, interview with church council, rehearsal for public profession of faith, and the worship ceremony.

Correcting Specific Behaviors

As we noted earlier, the area of social skills is one of the significant differences in persons with ASD. Sometimes an individual needs specific information, and this information can be conveyed in story form.

Perhaps a mentor would be willing to write a simple story for a friend. For example, if a church invites people to dance in front during worship, but an individual is not tuned in to the time that others will be going back to their seats, written information might be helpful. Simple stick figures and words written on a notecard might convey that it's time to dance. Another set of figures and words might tell the person to watch for a cue to sit down. For example, show a picture of another person who will be dancing and say, "When Jane sits down, you should sit down too." This simple tool conveys important information to make a friend feel comfortable.

At other times you may notice that an individual continues to make the same social error or blunder. For example, you might wish to write a story about how many questions one generally asks during a small group discussion or appropriate ways to touch another person during coffee time. These topics are generated by the needs of the individual with ASD.

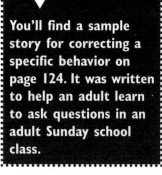

Expressing Faith in Jesus (© 2005, Faith Alive Christian Resources) is available from Friendship Ministries (1-888-866-8966 or www.friendship.org). This book and the accompanying kit for use in the preparation class were written for people with cognitive impairments, but the material could also be used with youth and adults with ASD. The emphasis on mentoring, use of visuals to explain biblical concepts for those with limited language, and ideas for using the gifts of each individual complement the strategies we've discussed in this book.

You'll find a sample story for correcting a specific behavior on page 124. It was written to help an adult learn to ask questions in an adult Sunday school class.

Sharing Information About a Person with ASD

Sometimes it's helpful to prepare a story about a person who struggles with verbal communication to share with others. For example, a parent or guardian may write a story about a child and share that story before the child first visits the library, goes to school or church, or plays at a neighbor's house. The story allows others to quickly understand that child.

We all like to share information about ourselves and experiences we have enjoyed. Children and adults with ASD can share their own story about a trip, their home and family, and so on with photo albums. Simple descriptive captions will help them tell the story so that others can enjoy their experience too. It's a conversation starter—just ask a grandma with pictures in her purse!

As you read over the story examples, you will notice that they are designed to give information. They are not in any way judgmental or punitive. They are not a list of rules, but a way to put social guidelines and expectations in writing. This is a powerful way to more fully welcome those with ASD into our faith community.

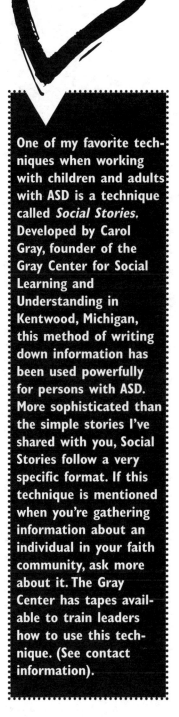

One of my favorite techniques when working with children and adults with ASD is a technique called *Social Stories*. Developed by Carol Gray, founder of the Gray Center for Social Learning and Understanding in Kentwood, Michigan, this method of writing down information has been used powerfully for persons with ASD. More sophisticated than the simple stories I've shared with you, Social Stories follow a very specific format. If this technique is mentioned when you're gathering information about an individual in your faith community, ask more about it. The Gray Center has tapes available to train leaders how to use this technique. (See contact information).

We've included a sample story about sharing information about a child with ASD on pages 125-126 in the reproducible resources section of this book. The story format is another way to share information with others who need to know and can be written from information gathered in an interview (see section 2 and sample interview questionnaires in the back of this book).

Strategy 10: Teaching Instead of Reacting

When I grasped the concept of teaching instead of reacting, my world as an educator and parent completely changed. So often we react to another individual's behavior with a consequence, lecture, correction, punishment, or pat phrase. Sometimes this is appropriate, but many more times when an individual acts in a certain way it's because he doesn't know what to do.

My least favorite time with my children sometimes occurs during a conversation we have after an incident:

> Son, why did you lose your computer time?
> Because you were upset with me.
> Son, why was I upset?
> I don't know.

My son is accepting the punishment, but he has no idea what he did wrong. That's when I know that I should have been using a teaching strategy instead.

For example, a child with ASD may come up to me and say, "You're fat." Although I'm working on that area of my life, it's the truth. We teach people to tell the truth, and yet my friend has just made a huge social blunder. Instead of sending that person to the corner chair or scolding that person, I might say, "You're right. But telling me that makes me feel sad. Let's just say hello to each other instead." We say hello and move on to the next thing. Instead of reacting, I just taught that individual what to do.

Many times in our interactions at church, we react by avoiding an individual. Instead of listening to Mary's story for the tenth time, we move away or find something else to do. When that happens, ask yourself, "What could I *teach* Mary so that we can have a pleasant conversation?" Perhaps you could carry in your pocket small notes that list topics of conversation. Have Mary choose one, and invite her to talk about this topic. This will teach Mary new ways of interacting with another person.

Although I could give dozens of examples, the best way to know when to use this strategy is to ask yourself this question: "Does the child or adult with ASD know what to do?" If not, then teach him or her a better way of responding. Even though you won't always have time to prepare for these teachable moments, remember to teach rather than react. I know my children appreciate it when I remember to follow this strategy! And the more familiar you become with the other strategies we've discussed, the easier it will be to teach.

Section 5
An Action Plan

Learning more about persons with ASD and developing strategies to meet their specific needs will do much to make your church a welcoming community for everyone. But this is not a one-time effort; rather, it is an ongoing ministry. The purpose of this final section is to equip you with the tools you need to create an action plan for your church and for the children and adults with special needs that God has placed in your faith community.

I recommend that you follow these ten steps:

Step 1. Share with your church your vision about including persons with special needs in the fabric of your congregation. Start with Scripture and the compelling evidence that God commands us to welcome all of his children as part of the body of Christ, including those with ASD. A pastor or guest speaker can address the issues raised in section 1: God's Handiwork.

Step 2. Recruit a coordinator for ministry to children and adults with special needs. You'll find a sample job description included on pages 127-128; for more on this task see page 100.

Step 3. Form a team or small group that will encourage the coordinator and help complete the tasks. (see pages 100-101).

Step 4. Provide training for the team. Offer books or videos or DVDs for self-study; attend conferences as a team. Consider partnering with an organization in your community that can offer training or consulting services. For a list of support organizations in the area of ASD and other special needs, see page 131.

Step 5. Develop a plan to *identify* individuals who may need extra support. You'll want to refer back to strategy 1 (pp. 41-48).

Step 6. Develop a plan to help support the individuals you've identified. It might include information from an interview (see strategy 1) and a profile of that person (see strategy 2) and culminate in an ISFP (Individual Spiritual Formation Plan—see p. 101).

Step 7. Follow up to make sure the plan is implemented and effective. Set check points and ways to evaluate progress.

Step 8. Offer ongoing support as needed by the individual and family. Needs change over time, and being proactive requires open communication.

Step 9. Use each individual's gifts in service to God as part of the body of Christ. Then ministry becomes *with* people with special needs rather than *to* them.

Step 10. Keep everyone aware and involved. This means you're committed to special needs ministry for the long haul.

Let's take a closer look at these four steps: recruiting a coordinator, forming a team, developing an Individual Spiritual Formation Plan, and keeping everyone aware and involved.

Recruiting a Coordinator

In previous sections I've emphasized the importance of recruiting a person to coordinate your ministry to children and adults with special needs, including those with ASD. Things will happen when one person's eyes are totally delighted by and fixed on including people who have special needs. Some churches have chosen to make this a part-time paid position; others recruit a volunteer.

The number one requirement for this position is having a heart for children and adults with disabilities. Although a degree in special education is not required, you'll want to look for someone who has the following attributes:

- good management and organizational skills.
- ability to network with a large number of people.
- some understanding of a wide range of disabilities.
- some understanding of techniques for working with children and adults who have disabilities.
- some understanding of where to obtain additional information and support.

Once this person is identified, you may want to set up a small group of people who can offer encouragement and advice and share some of the tasks of ministry.

Forming a Special Needs Ministry Team

Many churches have a worship team, an evangelism team, and a host of other service committees. Forming a team for ministry to children and adults with special needs will help to ensure that this ministry is focused and accountable.

Depending on the needs of your church, you may form a small group of people who serve as a support group for the coordinator or a more

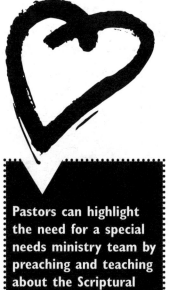

Pastors can highlight the need for a special needs ministry team by preaching and teaching about the Scriptural mandate we've discussed in section 1: God's Handiwork. The pastor's expression of God's heart for including everyone in the body of Christ will set the stage for forming a ministry team.

formal committee with members assigned specific roles. Perhaps one person could be in charge of initial contacts, another in charge of respite or family needs. Other assignments could include dealing with written publications or communications and acting as liaison to the church education program. Determine your ministry's specific needs, and set up a group of people dedicated to meeting these needs.

To equip the team, consider having them read this book along with *Helping Kids Include Kids with Disabilities* (© 2001, Faith Alive Christian Resources, 1-800-333-8300). Search your local library and the Internet for information about specific disabilities, and remember to use the expertise of individuals with ASD and their families. Special education programs and other services and programs in your local community are a good source of information. (You'll find a few such organizations listed on page 131-133.)

Developing an Individual Spiritual Formation Plan (ISFP)

In a school setting, a child with special needs is evaluated and then given a specialized program called an Individualized Education Program (IEP). An IEP lists what that child needs to have in place in order to be successful in school. It spells out goals and modifications that should be available for the child. For example, a child with a hearing impairment may need to sit near the front of class or have a teacher wear some type of microphone system. A child with a learning disability may be allowed to have all tests taken orally or have written material available on an audiotape. A child with Cerebral Palsy might need a special computer program used for writing or a special seat. The IEP spells out the child's specific needs, ways to meet those needs, who will be involved, and progress check points.

You'll find a sample ISFP form on page 129. You'll want to adapt the form to meet your needs.

In an effort to make our churches the five-star welcoming community God desires, I recommend developing an *Individual Spiritual Formation Plan* (ISFP) for each child or adult in your faith community who has a special need. Let's consider how this might work—first for a child and then for an adult.

Once you've identified a child or adult with special needs (strategy 1) and you've developed a profile to share with others (strategy 2), you are ready to develop a plan of action. Although this process will work for anyone with a special need, remember to think through the strategies that we have discussed when planning a successful program for a person with ASD.

If possible, gather together the people involved for a brief meeting. Perhaps parents or caregivers, the individual with ASD, the child's Sunday school teacher or adult's small group leader, a Friendship mentor, or special friend may want to be part of this planning meeting. The end result will be a form that outlines the Individual Spiritual Formation Plan (ISFP).

Keep this completed form on file, along with the interview questionnaire (or similar information-gathering device), profile, permission forms, and any other pertinent information for each person identified. Once this information is in place, make sure you get the parent's or individual's permission to share this information with others who need to know. (See sample permission forms on pp. 112-113.)

It's important that the coordinator commits to checking up on the plan, which is only a starting point. New strategies and ideas will evolve as the person with ASD becomes more involved in the church community.

Keeping Everyone Aware and Involved

Although I have highlighted this point throughout this book, I encourage you to make a specific plan to keep people aware and involved in your long-term ministry to those with special needs. Perhaps you will want to update the congregation as part of a newsletter or bulletin insert. Perhaps you will set aside a special announcement time a few times a year. Perhaps you will make a PowerPoint presentation or video of some of the things that are taking place. If your church has a website, make sure you include updates about this ministry. Encourage pastors and leaders to make inclusion a natural part of their preaching and teaching.

Once you have brainstormed a plan, write it down and check up on yourselves. Don't let months go by without letting everyone in your church family know that something exciting is happening. Let them know that your church really means "Everyone welcome!"

Whether you're just beginning a ministry to children and adults with Autism Spectrum Disorders and other special needs or whether you're looking for ways to make this ministry more welcoming, I trust this book will serve as a valuable resource. I encourage you to lean on God, our Father, who created each one unique; Jesus, our Savior, whose death and resurrection makes us members of the family of God; and the Holy Spirit, our helper, who gives us faith, insight, and gifts to serve God and others.

Reflections on Pastor Jared's Message

To summarize what I've wanted to convey in this book, I will share my reflections on a message by Jared Henderson, one of the pastors in my church. Pastor Jared's message was based on this passage from Hebrews 13:1-3:

> Keep on loving each other as brothers. Do not forget to entertain strangers, for by so doing some people have entertained angels without knowing it. Remember those in prison as if you were their fellow prisoners, and those who are mistreated as if you yourselves were suffering.

I challenge you to show three kinds of love.

- Show *passionate* love to those within the family of God. Our brothers and sisters come in a variety of packages, each unique. It's not our job to be the entry gate to the family—God has provided that through his Son, Jesus, and through the work of the Spirit in a person's heart. It is our job to unconditionally love each child or adult with ASD. It's that love which fuels plans and programs to allow each member of your community to be fully embedded and embraced within the body of Christ.

- Show *pursuing* love to those who are unfamiliar to you. Make sure each individual who comes through your church door truly understands that your church practices the invitation "Everyone welcome." You may be making that statement for the first time to a child or adult with ASD who has felt shunned and set aside by the church. Be aware that God may have given that person a gift that will richly bless your church. Who would want to miss this gift?

- Show *compassionate* love to those who suffer. Be willing to walk in the shoes of those who struggle the most so that you can best understand their gifts and needs. Instead of avoiding those whose lives are filled with disabilities and challenges that may have locked them out of the life in your church, be willing to get close.

As you minister to children and adults with ASD, hear God's promise: "Never will I leave you; never will I forsake you" (Heb. 13:5).

Let God's presence be the power that motivates, guides, and comforts you. Just as you place yourself beside a member of the body of Christ who has special needs, God places himself beside you. You'll never have a more faithful or powerful partner than your pursuing, compassionate, loving God.

Knowing that God is beside us gives us the confidence to say, "The Lord is my helper; I will not be afraid" (Heb. 13:6).

Perhaps you are being called to break new ground in your church community. Perhaps you have a vision for a way to be more loving within your particular congregation. Then go forward with confidence and with this blessing:

> *May the God of peace, who through the blood of the eternal covenant brought back from the dead our Lord Jesus, that great Shepherd of the sheep, equip you with everything good for doing his will, and may he work in us what is pleasing to him, through Jesus Christ, to whom be glory for ever and ever. Amen.*
>
> *—Hebrews 13:20-21*

Reproducible
Resources

- I Belong
- Sample Interview Questionnaire for Children's Ministry
- Sample Interview Questionnaire for Adult Ministry
- Sample Observation Form
- Sample Parent Permission Form
- Sample Adult Permission Form
- Story: Introducing Sunday School to Early Elementary Children
- Story: Introducing an Adult to a Small Group Bible Study
- Story: Explaining Changes in Programming
- Story: Describing Expected Behavior for Worship and Fellowship
- Story: Describing a Specific Event
- Story: Correcting a Specific Behavior
- Story: Sharing Information About a Child with ASD
- Sample Job Description for Coordinator of Ministry to Children and Adults with Special Needs
- Sample Individual Spiritual Formation Plan (ISFP)

These materials may be reproduced for local church use.

I Belong

For [God] created my inmost being; [God] knit me together in my mother's womb.
—Psalm 139:13

Let me tell you something about myself.

I am important to God. When God made me, God made me in his likeness. We are all made in God's image.
So God created man in his own image, in the image of God he created him; male and female he created them.

—Genesis 1:27

I belong to God's big family. Everyone who loves Jesus belongs to the body of Christ.
So in Christ we who are many form one body, and each member belongs to all the others.

—Romans 12:5

I am an important part of God's family in this church. We all have gifts to share with one another.
We have different gifts according to the grace given us.

—Romans 12:6

I have strengths and weaknesses. We all have strengths and weaknesses, but we can help each other.
Now to each one the manifestation of the Spirit is given for the common good.

—1 Corinthians 12:7

I have an Autism Spectrum Disorder. It's just a part of who I am. Each of us is one of a kind.
I praise [him] because I am fearfully and wonderfully made; [God's] works are wonderful, I know that full well.

—Psalm 139:14

Sample Interview Questionnaire for Children's Ministry

Child's Name: _____   Birthdate: _____

Parents' or Guardians' Name(s): _____   Phone: _____

Interviewer's Name: _____   Date: _____

1. What are your child's interests and strengths?

2. What things are difficult for your child?

3. Did you know at birth that your child might have some type of special need? How has your child's story unfolded?

4. Does your child have a diagnosis and/or educational label?

5. If you could choose three things that you hope could happen for your child this year at church, what would they be?

6. What suggestions do you have for your child's teachers and children's ministry leaders that may help them better include your child in the church education setting? (For example, sit closer to the teacher, assign a buddy each day, don't ask him to read aloud, avoid loud noises, and so on.)

7. Does your child have any medical conditions or medications that might be helpful for the leaders to know about? Please explain.

8. Will your child need any special help with personal care (using the bathroom, eating, getting dressed)? Please explain.

9. What would you like us to tell other children in the program with your child that will help them to better know, accept, and understand your child?

10. What other information might be helpful for us to know? (For example: favorite topics of conversation, food allergies, and so on).

Sample Interview Questionnaire for Adult Ministry

Name: _____ Birthdate: _____

Address: _____

Phone: _____ E-mail: _____

Interviewer's Name: _____ Date: _____

1. What are your interests and strengths? (For example: reading, music, drawing, cooking, computers, exercise, fishing, and so on.)

2. You indicated on our congregational survey that you have an area of special need. Please describe and explain how that affects your participation in the life of our church.

3. What things are you finding more difficult for you right now?

4. If you could choose three things you hope could happen for you at church this year, what would they be?

5. What suggestions do you have for the pastor and other leaders that may help them enable you to participate more fully in the life of our church? (For example, reserved or special seating in our worship service, visual aids, a mentor or friendship network, or a quiet area set up in the church.)

6. Do you have any medical conditions or medications that might be helpful for the pastor and other leaders to know about? Please explain.

7. What would you like us to tell the congregation to help them better know, accept, and understand you?

8. What other information do you feel might be helpful for us to know?

If someone other than the individual named completed this survey, please sign your name below and describe your relationship to the person named.

_____   _____

(name)   (relationship)

Sample Observation Form

Person Observed: _____

Time: _____ Place/Activity: _____ Date: _____

Observed by: _____

1. Activities and people this person seems to enjoy include

2. Activities this person did not seem to enjoy include

3. This person's body was calm and at rest when

4. This person's body and manner were agitated when

5. Based on this information, we might try

(Remember to observe this person again to see if what you tried was helpful).

Sample Parent Permission Form

I have read the attached profile about _____

(child's name)

prepared by _____.

(name and title)

I hereby give permission to distribute copies of this profile to those leaders who will be working with my child this year at _____.

(name of church)

This document should be treated as confidential, but the information may be used to better help the leaders understand how to work with my child.

At any time, I can ask for this profile to be returned to me and no longer distributed to the leaders. I must approve any other use of the material, such as in a church newsletter or other written form.

Signature: _____

Date: _____

Autism and Your Church, © 2006, Faith Alive Christian Resources, 2850 Kalamazoo Ave. SE, Grand Rapids, MI 49560.

Sample Adult Permission Form

I have read the attached profile describing my special needs prepared by

_____.

(name and title)

I give permission to distribute copies of this profile to the leaders who will be working with me this
year at _____.

      (name of church)

This document should be treated as confidential, but the information may be used to better help the
leaders understand me.

At any time, I can ask for this information to be returned to me and no longer distributed to the leaders.
I must approve any other use of the material, such as in a church newsletter or other written form.

Signature: _____

Date: _____

If someone other than the individual named is granting permission, please sign your name below and
describe your relationship to the person named.

_____   _____

(name)   (relationship)

Story: Introducing Sunday School to Early Elementary Children

Sunday school at Faith Church will begin on Sunday, September 6. I will meet new friends and learn more about Jesus.

First, we will meet in Room 10. Lots of kids will come to Room 10. We will sing praises to Jesus. Mr. Jackson will tell us what songs to sing.

Then each grade will go to their own rooms. Pastor Mary will slowly call out, "Kindergarten, First Grade, Second Grade, Third Grade." When I hear her say my grade, I will stand up and follow Mrs. Bentley to our classroom.

Mrs. Bentley has many things planned for us to do. We will hear a Bible story and pray together. We might make a craft, play a game, or do other things to help us learn about God

When we finish, Mrs. Bentley will take us back to Room 10. We can play games and have a snack.

Mom or Dad will pick me up in Room 10. When I see Mom or Dad at the door, it's time to go home. I'll wave goodbye to my friends.

Story: Introducing an Adult to a Small Group Bible Study

Adult Bible Study Starting Soon!

It's time for me to find a small group of people who know me and care about me. I can help them, and they can help me learn more about the Bible. I might like to join the adult Bible study this fall.

The Bible study will meet in Room 6 at church on Thursday nights at about 7:00 p.m.

Other adults will come to Room 6 too. First we will talk to each other and have coffee or juice.

The leaders, Annette or Ray, will greet us and ask us to sit down. Chairs will usually be set up in a semicircle.

We will study a book about angels. I can read the book myself, or I can read it with my mentor during the week.

We will talk about angels. I can share one thing I learned from the book. I can listen while others talk about what they've learned.

We will end by praying for each other. Ray will write our prayer requests on the board, and we will go around the circle to take turns praying for each other.

I can join this Bible study by calling Annette at 456-7890. She will mail me a list of the dates this class will be meeting. If I have any questions, I can ask Annette.

117

Story: Explaining Changes in Programming

Vineyard Summer Adventure

Children, get ready for an exciting summer at the Vineyard Adventure Park!

Each Sunday your parents will bring you to the table marked with blue, green, and yellow flags. They will help you get your summer adventure day pass and write your name on it.

Your pass will either be blue, green, or yellow. The color tells you where to start your adventure.

Blue

If your ticket is blue, go to the room with the blue door. When the weather is nice, you will play games and use chalk and bubbles outside. When it's rainy, you will play games inside.

Remember, you'll be safe outside when you play inside the fence. If you go outside the fence, you will need to go to the break area in the blue room.

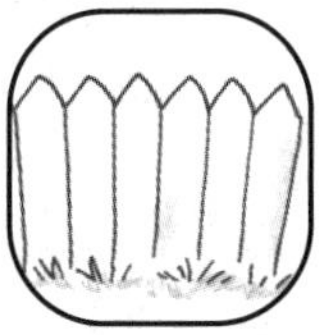

If your ticket is green, go to the room with the green door. This room has many surprises waiting for you.

Green

Yellow

If your ticket is yellow, go to the room with the yellow door. You will have fun creating your own things here.

When the bell rings, your leader will remind you to move to another room. By the end of each summer adventure day, you will have been in the blue room, the green room, and the yellow room.

Lots of moms, dads, and friends will be helping with our summer adventure. You can help by being a good listener and by being kind to others.

When you're helpful and kind in each room, the leader will stamp your Vineyard Adventure Park ticket. If you get all three stamps, you can choose a special treat to take home. Your family will be proud of you!

We hope you can join us every Sunday at the Vineyard Adventure Park!

If you want to know more about it, call Mrs. Barb at 456-7890.

Story: Describing Expected Behavior for Worship and Fellowship

Things You Might Like to Know About Calvary

We welcome anyone who wants to worship with us. We have morning worship for adults and teens in the room marked "Worship Center." People usually start sitting down in that room about 9:55 a.m. each Sunday.

Children are welcome at Calvary too! Children age four through those in grade 5 meet in the room marked "Children's Worship." A nursery is available for infants through age three. Children usually come about 9:50 a.m. each Sunday.

You'll see the information desk when you enter the church. A volunteer will answer your questions and help you find your way around.

Will we sing?

A worship leader will come to the front of the worship center when it's time to begin. Usually a group of two or three others will play piano, guitar, drums, or other instruments while we sing.

The words to the songs are shown on a large screen. You are welcome to sing along with the group. If you don't know the song, it's OK to listen and think about the words.

Will we greet others?

The people at Calvary enjoy being a part of the family of God and will want to welcome you. They will want to shake your hand. You will be invited to shake hands with the people around you too.

What should I wear?

The people at Calvary wear lots of different kinds of clothes. Some of the men wear a shirt and tie with dress pants; others wear casual shirts and pants. Some of the women wear dress-up clothes while others wear casual clothes.

People usually don't wear shorts to worship, but we'll welcome you no matter what you're wearing. We hope you'll find us all wearing smiles!

Every Sunday you'll find a bulletin on your chair in the worship center that explains the schedule for the morning. If you have other questions, a greeter or usher will be happy to talk to you and make you feel welcome.

Autism and Your Church, © 2006, Faith Alive Christian Resources, 2850 Kalamazoo Ave. SE, Grand Rapids, MI 49560.

Story: Describing a Specific Event
Celebrating Communion at Faith Church

The night before Jesus died on the cross, he ate supper with his disciples. When he served them the bread and wine, Jesus said, "When you eat the bread and drink the cup, remember me." Jesus wants us to remember that he gave up his body and blood to save us from our sins. That's why we celebrate communion at Faith Church.

All Christian churches celebrate communion. Some call it "the Lord's Supper." Churches celebrate communion in different ways.

At Faith Church, the pastor will read verses from the Bible and explain what communion means. You can listen quietly and think about what Jesus did for you.

Then the pastor will call three leaders to come to the table at the front of the church. These leaders are called elders. They will help the pastor serve the bread and grape juice.

The elders will first pass trays of broken bread. When the tray comes to you, you can take one piece and eat it. (You don't have to wait for everyone to eat the bread at the same time.) The pastor will remind everyone to think about what Jesus did for us when his body was nailed to the cross for our sins.

Finally, the elders will pass trays with small glasses of grape juice. When the tray comes to you, you can take one glass and drink it. (You don't have to wait for everyone to drink the juice at the same time.) Then place the empty glass in the holder. The pastor will remind everyone to think about what Jesus did when he shed his blood on the cross for our sins.

Autism and Your Church, © 2006, Faith Alive Christian Resources, 2850 Kalamazoo Ave. SE, Grand Rapids, MI 49560.

Story: Correcting Specific Behaviors
Asking Questions: A Guide for Adult Sunday School for Jolene

Jolene, welcome to adult Sunday school! Most people enjoy being a part of this group.

Often guest speakers will be invited to talk to the class. They might talk about things like the Bible, poverty, evangelism, and more.

People may want to ask the speaker a question. It's helpful if people raise their hand to let the speaker know they want to ask a question.

Remember, it's polite to give others a chance to ask a question, so it's best to ask only one question each week. It's OK to not ask any questions too.

Usually the speaker will ask if anyone has questions. Then it's a good time to ask the most important question.

Autism and Your Church, © 2006, Faith Alive Christian Resources, 2850 Kalamazoo Ave. SE, Grand Rapids, MI 49560.

Story: Sharing Information About a Child with ASD

My name is Joey Smith. My mom and dad want you to know more about me before I spend time with you.

I am five years old. My parents, Elise and Dave Smith, love me very much.

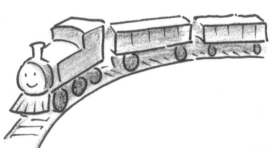

I like to do lots of things that other kids my age like to do. I like to play with trains and balls, and I'm very good at puzzles. Barney is my favorite TV character.

In a few ways, I am different from others kids who are five. I have autism.

If you ask me a question, I might repeat what you say. I can hear your words, but it's hard for me to answer questions.

Loud noises really hurt my ears! If I cover my ears or scream, just help me go to a quiet place. I will soon be calm again, and then I can come back to what I was doing.

It's really important for me to be with other kids and with adults. I need to hear others talk, and I can learn how to act around them.

It's important for others to be around me too. When they get to know me, they will see that I am also a child of God.

If you want to know more about me and about autism, just ask my mom and dad. They want to make sure that our time together is good for everyone!

Autism and Your Church, © 2006, Faith Alive Christian Resources, 2850 Kalamazoo Ave. SE, Grand Rapids, MI 49560.

Sample Job Description for Coordinator of Ministry to Children and Adults with Special Needs

In an effort to better welcome and include children and adults with special needs into the life of our church, Faith Church is seeking a person to coordinate this ministry. This person will be empowered and equipped to facilitate relationships between children and adults with special needs and their leaders, peers, and members of the church family. Beginning August 1st, the coordinator will assume a half-time paid position.

Qualifications

This person must express a heart for children and adults with special needs and possess

- good management and organizational skills.
- ability to network with a large number of people.
- some understanding of a wide range of disabilities.
- some understanding of techniques for working with children and adults who have disabilities.
- some understanding of where to obtain additional information and support.

Responsibilities

The coordinator will serve as the first point of contact for individuals and families and as the liaison between children and adults and others in the church family. To strengthen this ministry, the coordinator, along with a special needs ministries team, will

- develop a process for identifying children and adults with special needs who are members or who regularly attend Faith Church.
- gather information about each child and adult identified with special needs.
- in conjunction with the individual or family and based on information gathered, develop an Individual Spiritual Formation Plan (ISFP) that will allow the individual to be more fully involved in the life of the church.
- with the permission of the individual or family, share information with those who need to know, such as a child's or adult's leaders, peers, or the entire church family when deemed appropriate.
- oversee and implement each person's Individual Spiritual Formation Plan, monitoring its effectiveness on a long-term basis and changing or adapting the plan as needed.
- contact the individual or family at least four times throughout the year to make sure the plan is running smoothly.
- serve as chairperson of the special needs ministries team and together with the team
- be the "conscience" of the church for persons with disabilities.

- recommend additional staffing or special equipment based on the needs of particular individuals.
- offer information and training so that leaders, peers, and the church family may better include persons with disabilities.
- organize services such as respite care, parent support groups, and so on, as needed.
- look for opportunities for persons with disabilities to serve others within the congregation.
- submit an annual budget request and written summary of the ministry's accomplishments and goals to the church council.

Autism and Your Church, © 2006, Faith Alive Christian Resources, 2850 Kalamazoo Ave. SE, Grand Rapids, MI 49560.

Sample Individual Spiritual Formation Plan (ISFP)

Name: _____

Planning team participants: _____ Date: _____

Parent(s): _____

Facilitator: _____

Child's or adult's leaders (names and roles):

_____

_____

Others (names and relationship to child or adult):

_____

Areas of strength

Areas of difficulty

Physical accommodations (special seating, lighting, accessibility issues, break-time area, emergency call systems, sensory issues or needs, pencil with grip, and so on)

Staffing accommodations (co-teacher, assistant, nurse, one-on-one tutor, buddy, friendship network, and so o.)

Curriculum accommodations (material presented at a different level, review by parents, limited written work, no oral reading, shorter memory work, and so on)

Worship service accommodations (special seating, story schedules, visuals, parent assistance, presence of peer or mentor, and so on)

Important reminders (medications, emergency contacts and procedures, allergies, and so on)

Date for review of this plan _____

Autism and Your Church, © 2006, Faith Alive Christian Resources, 2850 Kalamazoo Ave. SE, Grand Rapids, MI 49560.

Recommended Resources

Organizations

Many organizations can provide information and support for your ministry to children and adults with autism. Those listed here are either specific Christian interdenominational organizations, they demonstrate qualities and a philosophy consistent with a Christian perspective, or they have products that a church might find helpful.

Ability Online
www.ablelink.org

> This Internet network allows kids with various disabilities to connect with others about issues related to their special needs.

Autism Society Canada
Box 22017, 1670 Heron Road
Ottawa, Ontario K1V 0C2
613-789-8943
Fax: 613-789-6985
www.autismsocietycanada.ca

CLC Network
4340 Burlingame SW
Wyoming, MI 49509
616-245-8388
www.clcnetwork.org

> This organization is dedicated to including persons with disabilities in the fabric of communities. Although the organization began its work with children in private schools, CLC Network now offers adult services as well as services to churches who want to set up educational programs and friendship networks (GLUE teams).

Friendship Ministries
2850 Kalamazoo Ave. SE
Grand Rapids, MI 49560
888-866-8966
friendship@friendship.org
www.friendship.org

Friendship Groups Canada
P.O. Box 27009
Kitchener, ON N2E 3K2
888-649-5555
Fax: 519-742-0614
info@friendshipgroupscanada.org

Friendship Ministries is an interdenominational, international ministry for people with cognitive impairments. Through consultation and with the help of resources that encourage spiritual development and relationships, Friendship Ministries helps churches to include people with cognitive impairments in fellowship and service as members of the body of Christ. This ministry, which is expanding to Hispanic churches in the United States and into Latin America, provides consulting, program support, and Bible study materials.

To request a list of Friendship curriculum materials, contact Friendship Ministries at 1-888-866-8966 or www.Friendship.org). If you're interested in starting a program, request the *Friendship Program Guide: A Resource for Leaders.*

Future Horizons, Inc.
721 West Abram Street
Arlington, TX 76013
800-489-0727
www.futurehorizons-autism.com

Future Horizons offers a catalog of materials exclusive to the field of Autism Spectrum Disorders. From children's books to resources for parents and professionals, this company is a primary resource for materials about ASD. They also offer conferences around the country for those who would like more information on ASD.

The Gray Center for Social Learning and Understanding
4123 Embassy Dr. SE
Kentwood, MI 49546
616-954-9747
www.thegraycenter.org

Although not a faith-based ministry, this organization demonstrates ideas and a vision that resonate within the Christian community. The Gray Center offers several excellent books and other resources, speakers, and conferences in the area of ASD. The center has information about Social Stories, a highly useful technique in the field of autism developed by Carol Gray, founder of the center. Center staff network with recognized experts in the field of ASD.

Time Timer
7707 Camargo Rd.
Cincinnati OH 45243
877-771-8463
www.timetimer.com

This company produces the visual timer suggested in these materials. It comes in a variety of sizes from one that fits in your pocket to a large display clock. No church should be without one!

Woodbine House
6510 Bells Mill Rd.
Bethesda, MD 20817
800-843-7323
www.woodbinehouse.com

Woodbine House offers materials exclusively focused on children who have special needs. In addition to children's books and adult resources in the area of autism, they offer resources on a large variety of disabilities.

Printed Resources

Again, this list is not exhaustive. It includes references referred to in this book and others you'll find helpful.

Abrams, Philip and Leslie Henriques. *The Autistic Spectrum Parents' Daily Helper.* Berkeley, Calif.: Ulysses Press, 2004.

Anderson, Neil T. *The Bondage Breaker.* Eugene, Oreg.: Harvest House Publishers, 1993.

Faherty, Catherine. *Asperger's: What Does It Mean to Me?* Arlington, Tex.: Future Horizons, Inc., 2000.

Gray, Carol. *The New Social Story Book.* Arlington, Tex.: Future Horizons Inc., 2000.

Kranowitz, Carol. *The Out-of-Sync Child.* New York: The Berkley Publishing Group, 1998.

Lockshin, Stephanie B.; Jennifer M. Gillis; Raymond G. Romanczyk. *Helping Your Child with Autism Spectrum Disorder.* Oakland, California: New Harbinger Publications, Inc., 2005.

Newman, Barbara J. *Helping Kids Include Kids with Disabilities.* Grand Rapids, Mich.: Faith Alive Christian Resources, 2001.

Pierson, Jim. *Exceptional Teaching: A Comprehensive Guide for Including Students With Disabilities.* Cincinnati, Ohio: Standard Publishing, 2002.

Shinsky, E. John. *Students with Special Needs: A Resource Guide for Teachers.* Lansing, Mich.: Shinsky Seminars, Inc., 1996.

Sohn, Alan and Cathy Grayson. *Parenting Your Asperger Child.* New York: Penguin Group, 2005.

Stuart-Hamilton, Ian. *An Asperger Dictionary of Everyday Expressions.* London: Jessica Kingsley Publishers, 2004.

The Easter Book: A Resource for Leaders and Mentors. Grand Rapids, Mich.: Faith Alive Christian Resources, 2003.

Twachtman-Cullen, Diane. *How to Be a Para Pro.* Higganum, Conn.: Starfish Specialty Press, 2000.

Vredeveld, Ronald C. *Expressing Faith in Jesus: Church Membership for People with Cognitive Impairments.* Grand Rapids, Mich.: Faith Alive Christian Resources, 2005.

Williams, Sondra. *Reflections of Self.* Kentwood, Mich.: The Gray Center for Social Learning and Understanding, 2005.